That's Why I'm Here is a touching tale of turning trouble into triumph through selfless giving in the face of harsh adversity. The story of Stefanie and Chris Spielman reminds all of us about how high we can rise even when fate tries to hold us down.

—MICHAEL A. CALIGIURI, MD, director of the Ohio State University Comprehensive Cancer Center and CEO of the Arthur G. James Cancer Hospital and Richard J. Solove Research Institute

THAT'S WHY I'M HERE

THE CHRIS & STEFANIE SPIELMAN STORY

CHRIS SPIELMAN

with BRUCE HOOLEY

ZONDERVAN®

ZONDERVAN.com/
AUTHORTRACKER
follow your favorite authors

We want to hear from you. Please send your comments about this book to us in care of zreview@zondervan.com. Thank you.

ZONDERVAN

That's Why I'm Here
Copyright © 2012 by Chris Spielman

This title is also available as a Zondervan ebook. Visit www.zondervan.com/ebooks.

This title is also available in a Zondervan audio edition. Visit www.zondervan.fm.

Requests for information should be addressed to:

Zondervan, *Grand Rapids, Michigan 49530*

Library of Congress Cataloging-in-Publication Data

Spielman, Chris, 1965–
    That's why I'm here / Chris Spielman with Bruce Hooley.
      p. cm.
    Includes bibliographical references and index.
    ISBN 978-0-310-33614-3 (hardcover : alk. paper)
    1. Spielman, Chris, 1965– 2. Football players—United States—Biography. 3. Sportscasters
—United States—Biography. I. Hooley, Bruce. II. Title.
GV939.S6397   2012
796.332092—dc23
[B]   2011050002

All Scripture quotations, unless otherwise indicated, are taken from The Holy Bible, *New International Version*®, *NIV*®. Copyright © 1973, 1978, 1984, 2011 by Biblica, Inc.™ Used by permission. All rights reserved worldwide.

Any Internet addresses (websites, blogs, etc.) and telephone numbers in this book are offered as a resource. They are not intended in any way to be or imply an endorsement by Zondervan, nor does Zondervan vouch for the content of these sites and numbers for the life of this book.

All rights reserved. No part of this publication may be reproduced, stored in a retrieval system, or transmitted in any form or by any means—electronic, mechanical, photocopy, recording, or any other—except for brief quotations in printed reviews, without the prior permission of the publisher.

Cover design: *Michelle Lenger*
Cover photography: *Amy Parrish*
Interior design: *Beth Shagene*

Printed in the United States of America

---

12 13 14 15 16 17 18 19 /DCI/ 24 23 22 21 20 19 18 17 16 15 14 13 12 11 10 9 8 7 6 5 4 3 2

To those who've battled cancer and to the survivors: you are not
alone in this fight.

To the doctors, nurses, researchers, and caregivers: continue to
devote yourselves to making this a cancer-free world.

To Maddie, Audrey, Macy, and Noah, in whose eyes I see the
strength, courage, grace, and honor of your beloved mother
every day.

CHRIS SPIELMAN
October 2011

To Mom and Dad: for showing me what commitment in marriage
truly means and for raising me in a Christian home.

To Sheri, Katie, Rachel, and Lexee: my cherished wife and
daughters and the proof that our Lord blesses us "exceedingly
abundantly above all we can ask or imagine."

To Chris, Maddie, Noah, Macy, Audrey, Myra, Sue, Cindy, and
Sandy: for allowing me the privilege of sharing the remarkable
story of your amazing wife, mother, daughter, and sister.

BRUCE HOOLEY
October 2011

CONTENTS

FOREWORD

Nobody ever said that life would be easy or that we will never experience hardships along the way. Many feel as if they can live life by going through the motions without stopping to think about what they have been given. For quite some time, I was one of those people. I stayed busy, whether with sports or schoolwork, and I often took things for granted. I just tried to get by in life and never thought anything severe could happen to me.

My wake-up call arrived in November 2009, after the passing of my mom. Her battle with cancer began in 1998, when I was four years old. She was always so selfless and determined to make sure we could live as normal a life as possible that, as a child, I often forgot anything was wrong with her health. My mom knew she had been allowed to have cancer for a specific purpose, and that purpose was to embrace God's plan for her life and help those who were going through similar circumstances. By participating in fundraisers and other charitable events over the course of her journey, my mom, along with the help of my dad, raised more than $9 million for cancer research.

My mom frequently spoke to groups of cancer survivors, always telling them not to be afraid and to trust what had been planned for each and every one of them. She gave hope to those who thought it no longer existed. Soon after my mom passed away, we received a letter from a woman my mom had spoken to several years earlier. In her letter, this woman told how she spoke to my mom to thank her for everything she had done to fight cancer and to give people hope.

My mom looked at her with surprise and, after a moment's hesitation, said, "Don't you understand? That's why I'm here."

That's Why I'm Here. And now you know the inspiration behind the title of this book.

My mom knew her purpose on this earth, and she welcomed the challenge with open arms. She lived one day at a time and never overlooked anything. Even in the darkest of days, I never heard her complain. She was, and still is today, my role model on how to live my life. I learned most everything I know from my mom. Even though the past two years have been very demanding emotionally, I truly believe that I have emerged as a stronger and better person.

In the future, I hope to continue my mom's legacy by supporting the fight against cancer and embracing the blessings and challenges that lie ahead. This entire experience has taught my family and me so much, but one thing is certain: I will never take anything for granted again.

MADISON SPIELMAN
October 2011

INTRODUCTION

I'VE HAD TWO GREAT LOVES IN MY LIFE. ONE WAS MY LOVE FOR MY wife, Stefanie. The other was my passion for my football career.

But my love for Stef vastly trumped the other.

Both loves play a large role in this book, and for that reason it may not look like any other book you've ever read. First, it's a book about Stef and my love for her, but especially about her courageous battle against breast cancer, a war she finally lost in November 2009. But it's also a book about football, a story about my obsession with the game from an early age through my career as a linebacker in the National Football League. Since the stories really can't be separated in our lives, they're both here in a combination that some people might think unusual. And so they might ask, "So, is it a football book?"

The answer is "Yes."

"Is it a love story, growing stronger in spite of terminal cancer?"

The answer is "Yes."

An unusual combination? I suppose so. And yet, the book is even more than that. Because at the core, it's really a story of faith in God, about how our loving heavenly Father weaves together the extremes of heartbreak and joy to create a new story that helps little boys grow up, grown women find their life purpose, and interested observers find new hope and deeper meaning in their own stories. The truth is, I can't tell you about any of these love stories without pointing to the spiritual foundation that both Stef and I shared. I promise I won't overwhelm you with it, but I have to be honest about how Stef and I weathered the serious challenges that came our way.

From the start, you need to know that Stef never viewed cancer as an unfair or undeserved penalty that took something away from her. She saw it instead as an opportunity to complete a mission that God had designed especially for her.

And from my side of things, I need to tell you how I gradually changed from being a prideful, self-willed professional athlete into becoming a man who has begun to understand and practice what it means to be a humble servant—and who, in the process, has become a better and a happier man because of it. For my entire NFL career, and for all the years before it when I devoted *everything* to reaching my goal of playing professional football, I never once imagined that what would come afterward could be so much more meaningful than any game or any season I ever played.

I'd been too wrapped up in trying to win the Super Bowl to think about the future.

I was too wrapped up in trying to be "the best" to consistently put others first.

But when doctors diagnosed Stef with cancer, everything changed. When a crisis like that levels you, it blasts you out of your comfort zone. Gradually, over what would become a twelve-year battle, Stef and I discovered together that God had shaped us for something much, *much* bigger than football. So please keep all of that in mind as you read the following pages. When you see a young boy so consumed with football that he can hardly think of anything else; when your jaw drops over a young man who went to all kinds of extremes to improve his game performance; when you are surprised at the all-out energy and focus a man would take to try and gain an edge over his opponents—I'd ask you to do me a favor.

Go ahead and laugh, cry, or question if you have to. But don't let it stop there. Understand that God has a burning passion for *you*, too, and that He can use your dreams, your desires, your passions for His plans, not just for yours—that He can also do something extraordinary in the lives of those around you.

For most of my life, I saw football as the ultimate destination of my journey. Instead, God used football to continually point me toward something else entirely.

And I believe He wants to do something a lot like that in your life, too.

CHRIS SPIELMAN
October 2011

CHAPTER 1

THE QUESTION

I ALWAYS LOVED THE LOCKER ROOM.

It's the one place on earth where nothing and nobody could ever bother me. It had been that way since before I played my first game of organized football, and that's how it was on October 20, 1997, as I prepared to play for the Buffalo Bills against the Indianapolis Colts on Monday Night Football.

I basically grew up in the locker room. My dad coached high school football, so I felt at home there from the time I started tagging along with him to practice as a toddler. I loved the sights, the sounds, the smells ... everything.

The locker room was my safe haven, my sanctuary.

Tonight, though, would be different.

Much different.

So different it would alter my life in a way I could not yet comprehend.

About five hours before kickoff, I sat alone inside our locker room, preparing to do the job I loved. I'd sat in locker rooms like this my whole life. It's where I felt most at home, most alive, because football consumed my life and gave order to everything I did. From the time I could formulate my first thoughts of what I wanted to become, I always gave the same answer: a football player.

Early in my career, I told an interviewer, "This is my life: I grow up. I play football. I play in the NFL. I retire. I coach football. I die." That shallow and self-absorbed approach defined me, and at the time I completely embraced it as the way to be the best at what I did.

Other boys wanted to become cops or firemen or doctors. Not me. I wanted to be a professional football player. If I couldn't become an NFL player, then I wanted to become a garbage man, because I thought it would look cool to ride around hanging on the back of that big truck.

Given where I grew up, it seemed my destiny to play football at the highest level. After all, I was born in Canton, Ohio, where professional football began in the 1920s with the Canton Bulldogs and the legendary Jim Thorpe. The National Football League began in Canton and later the Professional Football Hall of Fame was built there, just a mile from the house where I grew up. Located in northeast Ohio, Canton sits next to Massillon, perhaps the No. 1 high school football town in America. Massillon has a football stadium that seats 17,000— over half the town's population of 30,000. They named the stadium after the legendary Paul Brown, who coached high school football in Massillon before he became the father of modern professional football with the Cleveland Browns.

Every baby boy born in Massillon receives a tiny orange-and-black football in his crib from the nurses at the hospital. Maybe that's why the Massillon Washington Tigers have won twenty-two state championships and more games than all but two high school programs in America.

I wasn't born in Massillon, but football was born into me. My dad took me and my older brother, Rick, to practice with him from the time we could walk. While other kids watched cartoons or Saturday matinees, I watched game films with my dad and his coaching staff. I learned not just to watch the game but to see the game, to understand how it unfolded and, most importantly, to admire the same qualities in a player that my dad valued most.

He loved tough, relentless, passionate, hard-hitting guys, and so I came to love that style too. I channeled all my energy into becoming a physical, aggressive player. When I got my first football helmet for Christmas at age five, my grandma came over to the house. "Hey, Chris," she said, "you wanna play some football?" I tackled her right there in our living room. I mean, I took her out. She bounced right up, though. You could tell she was a Spielman.

Whatever toy I had—a GI Joe, army men, cowboys—they all became football players. I loved crashing them into each other like the collisions I saw on the field. I fantasized about becoming that kind of player, and I became exactly that. I understood the violence inherent in football, and I played it violently, within the rules. The position of linebacker fit my skills and my temperament like a glove. Launching your body at a high rate of speed into other human beings, with no regard for anyone's safety (yours or theirs), requires an indifference to physical pain. Since linebackers must do that, I did that—and I loved doing it.

That night in Indianapolis, I prepared myself to do it again.

Some players will tell you they get more motivated to play on Monday night because of the national television audience and because most every player in the NFL tunes in. That causes them to put a little extra into their preparation for Monday night games. I didn't need any extra incentive because I prepared the same for every game, every year, whether at Massillon, at Ohio State, or in the NFL.

I tailored my preparations that night to eliminate anything that might catch me off guard. I pored over every detail in the scouting report to remove, as much as possible, the chance of letting my team down because I called the wrong defense, failed to make the right adjustment at the line of scrimmage, or missed some minor detail that might make the difference between victory and defeat.

In order to do that, I had my own pregame routine that allowed me to get into the proper frame of mind. For home games that started at 1 p.m., I woke up at 6:30 a.m. and arrived at the stadium by 7 a.m. On road trips, I didn't wait for the team bus. I took a cab and arrived hours ahead of the rest of the guys just so I could feel the stadium. I know it sounds weird, but I wanted to absorb the atmosphere, soak it in, and build toward a mental peak necessary to perform at a high level.

That night in Indy, like every other game I played, I arrived at the stadium before any of my teammates. I slipped into my football pants more than four hours before kickoff so I could get accustomed to them, so they felt like a part of me by the time I needed to bring a nasty attitude to the field.

I started downing as much coffee as I could and tried to offset the dehydration the caffeine brought on by pounding as much Gatorade as possible. I read whatever book I had at the time for maybe twenty minutes before I got too jittery from the coffee to continue. Then I took one more look at the previous week's game film of the Colts, just one final check to make sure I hadn't missed anything.

I invented my own way of watching film. I cleared all the chairs in the room to one side and held the clicker in my hand as I watched the view taken of the entire field from behind the defense. Linebackers see the game from that perspective. Through visualization, I projected myself into the film and became the linebacker for the team playing our next opponent. Many times, what I visualized while watching film happened in the game and prepared me to jump on it.

Like everything I did, I took visualization to the extreme. I always felt if I could get myself angry to play, get myself into a bad mood, then I would bring a little bit extra to knocking people down as hard as I could. I knew on the other side of the building, in my opponents' locker room, they had bad intentions for me. So I made sure a regular part of my routine included working myself into a lather before I went out on the field.

As I worked myself into this frenzy—while going to the bathroom for about the eighth time (remember the coffee and the Gatorade) —I began thinking, *It's time. Let's go. It's what you've been put on this earth to do.*

Then, all of a sudden, out of nowhere, I got this message, this voice in my head, this overwhelming feeling of a question:

"Chris, what is your purpose on this earth?"

I shook it off. I distinctly remember saying out loud, "I don't need this right now."

Back into my routine, I stretched, warmed up, and went over last-minute preparations with the defensive line and the secondary, making sure they knew what we would adjust to, depending on the look the Colts gave us at the line of scrimmage. Just before going out onto the field for kickoff, I did what I always did—I broke two smelling salts capsules and shoved one up into each of my nostrils.

Now, with a clear head, I joined our other captains for the walk to midfield for the pregame coin toss. But as I got to the spot between the numbers and the hash marks, here came that question again, only stronger this time:

"Chris, what is your purpose on this earth?"

I don't know why it came. It had never happened before. I had always been able to focus on the task at hand and immerse myself in the game. So, after the coin toss, I screened out the question and began doing what came naturally.

We held a 6–3 lead entering the fourth quarter, but the Colts started driving downfield. They handed off to Lamont Warren on a run up the middle, and I had a clear, clean shot at him. That's rare in the NFL. Usually someone blocked me or at least chipped at my knees or ankles. It didn't happen often that I got the chance to unload on someone without anybody in my way.

When I got those opportunities, I didn't waste them. No NFL player will respect you if you shy away from slamming someone when given the chance. If I ever saw anyone shy away or turn down serious contact, that player had absolutely no credibility with me. I vowed I would never be one of those guys. I never had been, and I wasn't going to start now, with Lamont Warren coming right at me.

So I blasted him. On most of my good hits in the NFL, I'd feel it. It would hurt, but the pain never bothered me. I actually liked it. But this time, I lay on the field after making the tackle and couldn't feel anything. I don't mean I couldn't feel anything, like when your driver mushes against a golf ball on a drive you really crush. I mean, I didn't feel *anything*. Not in my arms, not in my legs, not anything. I couldn't move for about five or six seconds. Because of the momentary paralysis, I stayed down longer than normal. But, finally, like the feeling you get when you hit your crazy bone or when your foot or hand falls asleep, my body began tingling and I regained the strength to get up before the trainers came out to take a look at me.

I thought, *Boy, that was weird*, but I didn't come out of the game. We ended up winning, 9–6, on a field goal as time expired.

Afterward, the happiness I felt over winning didn't erase the nagging concern over what happened on that hard hit in the fourth quarter. Coming clean about it, telling the doctors, would mean medical tests and maybe missing games, so I just blew it off. Why risk that? After all, I played the rest of the game. I must be OK. I hated the idea of going on injured reserve. To that point in my career, I had started every game but four. If I had my way, I wouldn't have missed those, but they put me on the injured reserve list while I was on the operating table for a shoulder injury (that I fully intended to play with).

I didn't want to risk giving up my spot in the lineup, so I didn't tell the doctors or anyone what happened to me. In my heart, I knew I shouldn't ignore it. It bothered me enough that when I got on the team bus for the ride to the airport, I said something to a teammate, Tim Tindale.

"Man, when I hit that guy in the fourth quarter, I didn't feel anything. I was paralyzed for a second. Did that ever happen to you?"

Tim played special teams. He earned his spot on the roster because of his all-out approach. He flew around out there like a crazy man, so his answer didn't surprise me. "Oh, yeah," he said. "That happens. Don't worry about it."

So, with my rock-head mentality and not wanting to admit I might have seriously injured myself, I didn't think any more about it. I went through practice the next week without any symptoms and prepared to play the Denver Broncos at home in Buffalo.

Three more times in that game I got the same feeling, those slight bouts of paralysis. I never stayed down long enough for the trainers to come on the field, and I'd grown used to it by now. But in my heart I understood the seriousness of the situation. Despite hitting thousands of guys over the years, this had never happened to me before. I'd never had so much as a concussion, at least that I knew of. But now I had lost all feeling in my body four times in seven days. *Something* had to be wrong.

After getting dressed, I walked up the steps from the locker room in Rich Stadium to where the players' wives gathered. I got to the top of the stairs and saw Stef across the room. The second I saw her, I knew I couldn't ignore the problem anymore. I took one look at her and walked back down the stairs to see the doctor. I told him what happened, and he made arrangements for me to get tested the next day.

Two weeks later, I was in bed at Christ Hospital in Cincinnati after surgeons removed a herniated cervical disc pressing on my spinal cord. That had caused the paralysis. Whenever the disc brushed the cord, I'd momentarily lose all feeling. The doctors fused my third and fourth vertebrae.

They called the surgery a success but wouldn't guarantee that I could continue playing in the NFL. I lay there thinking, *This might be it. I might have the chance to come back, but this might be it.* The anesthetic from surgery had me pretty loopy, so I drifted in and out of sleep deep into the night.

Then I woke up and I heard it again—that same burning question from the Monday night game in Indianapolis:

"Chris, what are you doing? What is your purpose on this earth?"

This time, I couldn't get it out of my mind. I had no game to play. I had nothing to distract me. Confined to that bed, I had no place to go and no physical ability to get there even if I had an escape route. So I gave the same answer I gave before: "Hey, I've already addressed that. I'm not dealing with that question now."

It didn't occur to me that this question might have come from God trying to get my attention. I grew up in a Catholic home, and we always went to church as a family. I knew the importance of serving God; it just wasn't as important to me back then as football. At Ohio State, Stef and I attended Fellowship of Christian Athletes meetings, where I got the answers to why I believed what I believed. But I quickly moved on to, "OK, when's the next football practice?" I didn't suddenly start submitting to God every day. I still thought I had most of the control over my life.

When I got out of the hospital in Cincinnati, I spent time resting and recovering at home in Columbus, where Stef and I had moved our family the year before, after I signed as a free agent with the Bills. My rehabilitation progressed well. I worked out regularly at Ohio State and my neck felt good. The Bills scheduled a mini-camp for June, which I planned to attend. I hadn't been cleared to fully participate yet, but I wanted at least to get out there and do movement drills to show them I could come back and play the 1998 season.

Stef was pregnant at the time and, man, did that excite us. We had our third child on the way, and I was preparing to make the Comeback Of The Century. While I knew my comeback wasn't really *that* big of a deal, I approached everything that way. Whatever I did or planned to do, I made it into the biggest thing ever to happen to anyone, just to motivate myself. I invented doubters that didn't exist, just to fire myself up. As I recovered and trained, I told myself that not only would I play again, but I'd play better and with a bigger chip on my shoulder than ever before.

Back then, nothing quenched my thirst for perfection. No matter what I accomplished, it was never enough. I always reached for the next thing. I always wanted more. I remember writing down, prior to my senior year at Ohio State, "Never be satisfied or content. Always want more. That way, you'll always compete more." I felt that if I ever became satisfied or content, I wouldn't compete enough and I'd lose my edge.

I absolutely needed a mental edge on everyone. Some way, somehow, I would get it. I taught myself—brainwashed myself, really—to reject the very idea of satisfaction. Even if my team had won the Super Bowl, I would have refused to rest or enjoy it for long. I always would have wanted more.

That single-minded devotion to football bled over into my marriage. Nothing could detract in any way from what I felt kept me at my competitive best. Stef never protested. She understood my obsession, and she realized that the same obsession made me a good husband and father. She knew that my drive to "be the best" meant I also took my duties in the home seriously.

But most of all, she knew that I loved her with all my heart. The first time I ever laid eyes on Stefanie, I thought she was the most beautiful woman I had ever seen. We'd been together ever since our first date at a high school dance in Massillon, when she was fifteen and I was seventeen. I cherished her as my wife and I dearly loved Maddie and Noah.

But still, our lives revolved around me.

Whatever we did as a family had to fit into my preparations for football. Nothing could intrude. I told Stef, "I'll go anywhere you want to go on vacation, but we can't be gone too long, and wherever we go has to have a good weight room so I can work out." *My* priorities came first.

That summer, while I worked my way back into shape after my spinal fusion surgery, Stef miscarried our baby. That just leveled her emotionally. While I tried my best to help her through the pain, I focused more on my comeback. I set my mind on getting back to the NFL. I focused *everything* on that.

After the miscarriage, Stef told her gynecologist, Dr. Bill Copeland, about a lump she discovered in her breast during the pregnancy. She hadn't said anything before then because she thought her out-of-whack hormones maybe explained the lump. But Dr. Copeland called the lump abnormal and recommended Stef get a mammogram.

At that time, I thought, *This can't be anything. God certainly isn't going to disrupt this tremendous comeback I'm about to make. We'll get the mammogram. It will be nothing, and we'll try again for a third child.*

Stef went in for the test on a Friday afternoon, alone. It was supposed to be just a routine procedure, so I didn't go with her. But that morning, July 7, I woke up with an anxious feeling. *Real* anxious. *This isn't right*, I thought. *Something is wrong.*

Leaving to work out didn't help me relax. Normally, I treated every workout with the same intensity I did a game. I cleared my mind and focused intently on getting the most out of my training. But that day, I couldn't concentrate at all. I had this feeling of dread that I just couldn't shake.

When Stef came home, I asked how the test went. "OK," she said, but at that point, I reflected on two nights earlier, before she had the mammogram, when she showed me the lump. Its massive size shocked me. It seemed as big as a golf ball. When she told me the test went OK, I got a mental picture of the size of that lump. I had a sick feeling that this meant big trouble, but I also deluded myself with the thought: *God is going to take care of this. God wants me to be a football player.*

About 1:30 or 2 p.m. that afternoon, the phone rang. Maddie and Noah were taking their naps. Stef answered the phone in our kitchen. The doctor began going over the test results. I stood right beside her, and although I couldn't hear every word he said, I could clearly see Stef's facial expression and read her body language. They didn't talk long. They didn't need to. What can a doctor say in that situation but to give you the truth and give it to you straight? I knew what her reaction meant. My worst fears had come true. She had breast cancer.

We just stood there in the kitchen, holding each other. The news leveled us. The feelings—fear, dread, uncertainty—washed over us. Neither of us knew what to say. Stef showed more outward emotion than I did only because I tried to put up the strong husband front, assuring her we would get through this together. But inside it ate me up. It felt like someone took a bat and beat me to a pulp.

We spent the rest of the afternoon in a fog. Eventually, we got someone to watch Maddie and Noah so we could go in for our first appointment with the cancer doctors. The silence on the short drive to the hospital only added to the surreal nature of what we'd learned only hours before.

Finally, I just couldn't take it anymore. I pulled up to a stop sign at Kinnear Road and North Star Road, preparing to turn right and head to the cancer hospital on the Ohio State campus. The emotions, the frustration, the anger, the helplessness, the rage just welled up inside me and came pouring out. I started punching the steering wheel, cussing, screaming: "WHY IS THIS HAPPENING TO US? WHAT THE @#$#@%^#$ IS GOING ON AROUND HERE? FIRST MY NECK AND NOW THIS. IT'S NOT FAIR!"

I kept punching and screaming until Stef shouted at me, "STOP IT!"

I'd rarely heard her use that tone with me, but she didn't stop. She looked right at me, almost through me, and said, "How *dare* you?"

I didn't know how to reply. "What are you talking about?" I asked.

She looked at me with fierce determination and said, "How dare you say those things with all the blessings we've been given in our life?"

That humbled me to no end and I instantly realized I had disappointed her. I had let her down.

In silence we went in to meet with the doctor, where we heard the words no one wants to hear, words we would hear all too often over the next twelve years—words that would become a way of life, and death, for us.

"Tumor ... malignant ... metastasized ... cancer."

I listened, half in a daze, trying to ask the right questions, trying desperately not to let down this amazing, vibrant young wife and mother—the only woman I'd ever dated, let alone loved—whose mortality now stood out very clearly at the age of thirty.

We found out what we needed to do to fight back. We didn't know if the cancer had spread, but we knew we would battle with everything inside us. I walked out, thinking, *We'll heal from this and head back to Buffalo for the season.*

But driving home, guess what thought came burning into my mind?

"Chris, what is your purpose in life?"

This time, I had an answer.

CHAPTER 2

THE ANSWER

I DOUBT ANYONE COULD LOVE FOOTBALL MORE THAN I DID, BUT I always knew I loved something else more. Stef and our children truly were more important to me than the game that most everyone believed ranked first on my priority list.

Stef completely captivated me in a way football never could. I wanted to be with her every moment. I'd never felt that way about anyone before I met her, and my love for her deepened every day.

Her diagnosis gave me the chance to sacrifice for her the way she had always sacrificed for me throughout our marriage. I thought back on every interview for every feature story written about me over the years. The writers consistently focused on my complete immersion in the game and my overwhelming desire to be the best. I routinely said in those interviews that despite the emphasis I placed on my profession, my wife and children ranked far ahead of football on my priority list.

Now, my moment of truth had arrived. I couldn't say that being a husband and father trumped everything else if, when given the chance to demonstrate my love for Stef, I ran in the other direction. So the answer to the question, "Chris, what is your purpose in life?" became obvious. I would serve God, serve my family, and serve the community. I didn't know everything that would mean, but I knew that's where it all began.

Even as a kid, I had a very clear distinction between right and wrong. Along with that came an equally clear sense of duty to do the right thing, according to my beliefs. And the same obsession that

fueled my desire to be the best in football—the same single focus
and drive—also fueled my determination to do the right thing and to
stand up for the underdog.

In fourth or fifth grade, when I was nine or ten, I remember riding the school bus one day when some kids started making fun of a
few mentally handicapped students. That made me really mad, and I
remember standing up for the handicapped students, sitting by them,
and letting the other kids on the bus know, *Don't mess with them or
you'll have to mess with me.* I was always a big kid, and as an athlete
I became pretty popular; and I figured that if my classmates saw me
standing up for the underdogs, they might respect that and maybe
even follow my actions. I don't remember that anyone bothered those
kids again.

Beyond the bus incident, I recall often going out of my way to talk
to the "unpopular" kids in school, and to make sure they got included
in various activities. In fact, it became almost a natural instinct for
me. I suppose that both my makeup and upbringing steered me into
becoming a kind of "protector" or "fix it" guy.

Maybe this stemmed from my dad's discipline and the knowledge
that I'd get punished for doing something wrong. Maybe some of it
came from the lessons I learned in athletics, that without hard work
and the proper training, I wouldn't succeed. And some of it probably
traces to the blue-collar, hard-working spirit of the area where I grew
up in northeast Ohio.

While I don't know exactly where my approach came from, I do
know it shaped how I viewed and reacted to *everything.* I developed
this code, which dictated how I conducted myself and how I lived.
Work hard, tell the truth, do good, defend the weak, sacrifice for
others—all of it became part of that code. No one told me about the
code or pressured me to do things in a certain way. I invented the
code for myself and I enjoyed living by it. It appealed to me more and
more because I had success following it. Since every success drove me
deeper into that mind-set, I added to my code over time. I didn't know
any other way to live, and I didn't *want* to know any other way to live,
because I figured if I strayed from my code, I would not succeed.

Ever since I can remember, I wanted to become an NFL football player. As I got older, I also realized I wanted to have a great marriage and a wonderful family. Now I had all those things—so why would I jeopardize any of it by straying from the code? Instead, my code became stricter as the years passed. I *liked* living that way. I *liked* knowing that no other player worked harder than me and that other players wouldn't do what I did to prepare.

At one of our first team meetings in Buffalo, Marv Levy stood up and said, "Men, you have to be willing and able to go where your opponent is unwilling and unable to go." I sat there and thought, *Well, I already do that. What else do you have for me, Coach? Give me the next thing.* As I looked around that locker room, I had complete certainty that I already had gone where none of the rest of those guys had been willing to go.

But the challenge of breast cancer was more difficult than anything I'd ever faced in football. Although neither Stef nor I had any idea what lay ahead, I believed that question—"What is your purpose in life?"—came directly into my heart and mind to prepare me to move the focus from myself to Stef.

If you have any sort of spiritual side, times of extreme crisis prompt you to focus more on God. "Why are You allowing this to happen? Please heal my wife. Help me to be strong for her and our kids." That's how I prayed. But I didn't yet have a complete understanding of serving God.

In the same way, neither Stef nor I comprehended what her breast cancer battle would turn into. We couldn't have known in the first days after her diagnosis how completely the public would embrace her battle. We didn't fathom how much other cancer patients' stories of survival would inspire and strengthen us. Nor did we expect that the way we tackled breast cancer would impact others.

All of that developed from God's divine hand steering us through the ups and downs of treatment.

But on July 9, 1998, the day we drove to the hospital for Stef's first appointment, we thought only about the mastectomy she would have six days later to remove (we hoped) all the cancer and beat the disease forever.

I tried to put on a brave front. I didn't want my mind-set to give Stef any concern or add to her burden. But inside, worry consumed me. I raced through every scenario of what might happen. We didn't talk much about the worst possible outcome because neither of us wanted to go there, but I thought about it constantly and I'm sure she thought about it too.

We both leaned hard on our faith for comfort and inspiration. That always had been an element of our relationship from the time we started dating. I grew up in a Catholic home and Stef was Presbyterian, but that denominational difference never caused an issue between us or our families as we fell in love and got married.

We began to mature in our reliance upon Jesus Christ as our Savior when we attended Bible studies together, first at Ohio State and later in Detroit during my first eight years in the NFL. I genuinely desired God's presence in my life, but my devotion lacked something in those days. I knew the importance of serving God, according to my code. But submission to God, yielding to His will and not imposing my own —*that* level of faith I didn't yet fully comprehend.

You can think you have a mature faith, but trials test the strength of your faith in a way the good times in your life cannot. At those times, you either run to God or you run away from God. But even though Stef and I ran to God, making that choice didn't free us from anxiety or concern. One of our favorite Scriptures, Philippians 4:6–7, says, "Do not be anxious about anything, but in every situation, by prayer and petition, with thanksgiving, present your requests to God. And the peace of God, which transcends all understanding, will guard your hearts and your minds in Christ Jesus." Despite the comfort that passage brought us, we knew our faith didn't guarantee us an earthly healing for Stef. We prayed for and hoped for the best, while trying to prepare for the worst.

We knew we needed to prepare Maddie and Noah for the surgery. Stef and I both felt strongly that it would be wrong to lie to them or mislead them in any way. They deserved to know—but only what they could understand. How do you explain cancer to kids who are four and two? Stef told them, "Mommy has a boo-boo on her boobie, and the doctors need to take it out." Then she told them she might have to take some icky medicine that would make her feel yucky, but that Grandma would be coming to stay with us for a while to help out. Once they heard the last part, they were fine.

It amazed me how bravely Stef approached the whole run-up to surgery. Almost immediately, just as she did in the car on the way to the hospital that first night, she accepted the reality handed to her and resolved to face it head-on. She wrote this in her journal two days after her diagnosis:

> *I do not feel sorry for myself. I do not wish this would have happened to anyone else. I know that I will be thrown for a loop initially, but I pray I will grow stronger with each passing day. I cannot let this get the best of me and I will not let this ruin the rest of my life — no matter how long it is.*

Still, she walked into the Arthur G. James Cancer Hospital for surgery on July 15 feeling considerably anxious and uncertain. She didn't want to be there and neither did I, but we also knew we couldn't avoid it. Dr. William Farrar, the chief of surgical oncology, would perform the operation. He made us no promises. We knew from talking to him that breast cancer, when detected at Stage I, had a 15 percent chance of recurring. At Stage II, the chance rose to 20 to 30 percent. At Stage III, it increased to 50 percent, and at Stage IV the cancer returned with 80 percent certainty.

We wouldn't know which stage applied to Stef until after the surgery, and even then we had no guarantees. We learned that breast cancer cells can migrate anywhere in the body — to the brain, the spine, the lungs, the bones — but often they go undetected for years after they travel from the breast to some other place. The tumor in Stef's breast alerted us to the problem, but those cells might have been there up to five years before they took the form of a tumor. They might already have moved elsewhere in her body without yet showing up.

We hoped the cancer cells had confined themselves to her breast.

Once Dr. Farrar removed them, we hoped they wouldn't return. We clung to the hope of Stef being among that fortunate 85 percent of patients where the cancer gets caught at Stage I and never returns. Had we known then what awaited us over the next twelve years—the peaks and valleys of treatment, the innumerable trips through those doors of the Arthur G. James Cancer Hospital—we probably would have sprinted out of there. Instead, I kissed her as they took Stef away for surgery. Then I walked to the waiting room and began praying, "Please, don't let it be anything. Please, don't let it be anything. Please, don't let it be anything."

Sometimes when you feel desperate, your prayers lack eloquence. Mine came out pretty primitive. Despite my wish for more spiritual prayers, my heart dictated the only words I could muster.

I sat there and waited, hoping the doctors would catch it all in time, that Stef would heal from surgery, that we'd head off to Buffalo for my comeback so our lives could return to normal. Maybe it would all end up just a horribly bad scare.

Dr. Farrar raised my hopes with his first words after surgery. He said he removed Stef's right breast and the lump inside, which revealed pre-cancerous or pre-invasive cells, indicative of a Stage I tumor. But after that great news came devastating news. He also found another tumor near her chest wall, indicating the cancer had spread. For that reason, he also removed twenty-eight lymph nodes for further examination. He explained that lymph nodes serve as a filtration system for the blood. They catch rogue cells attempting to travel elsewhere in the body. If the cancer showed up in her lymph nodes, that would be extremely bad news. It would mean the cancer had tried to migrate. It might hide in her lungs, her spine, her brain ... anywhere. Or it could remain confined to the lymph nodes. Regardless, if they found evidence of cancer in the lymph nodes, Stef would definitely need chemotherapy.

Both of us desperately wanted to avoid that. We'd heard the horror stories of what chemo did to your body. So I sat there in the recovery room, waiting for Stef to wake up, knowing I would have to tell her about that second tumor and the removal of the lymph nodes. It's one of the toughest things I've ever had to do, and one of the things that breaks my heart to this day.

As soon as she opened her eyes, the first thing she said was, "Please, Chris, no more surprises. Tell me there are no more surprises."

It took everything I had not to break down right there. I just said, "Don't worry. Get some rest. We'll talk to the doctor."

I drove home that night feeling helpless. The doctors had yet to test the lymph nodes, but they cautioned me that from the feel of them, they believed Stef's lymph nodes contained small tumors. I couldn't sleep. I struggled with how to tell Stef the bad news about her lymph nodes ... and something else ate at me too. Thoughts began nagging me about my response to what might lay ahead.

I put all of that aside until we met with the doctors the next day. I wanted to remain positive. I tried not to expect the worst. Maybe we would get a miracle.

Instead, they told us the results showed evidence of cancer in two of the twenty-eight lymph nodes. She would need chemotherapy.

This nightmare kept getting worse.

Some nurses came in to give us the chemotherapy details. Stef listened intently, shaken by their explanation of the side effects. She would lose her hair. She would feel sicker than she'd ever felt. She would have almost no energy, and her mind might not work as sharply as it had. All of these things would be "temporary"—as if six months of poison getting pumped into your body could ever be considered temporary.

The doctors and nurses couldn't answer any of my questions about whether they'd removed all the cancer from Stef's body, whether it had spread anywhere else, whether we could count on a cure once chemo ended.

I already knew the answer to what the future held, or didn't hold, for me. Training camp in Buffalo would start at the end of the month. I'd looked forward to the opportunity to prove I'd recovered from neck-fusion surgery the previous November. I wanted to reclaim my old spot at linebacker. But now that I knew Stef faced chemotherapy, I knew I couldn't go to Buffalo. I needed to put my football career on hold and take care of my wife for as long as she needed me. So I resolved not to play the 1998 season. I would stay home with Stef, care for her during treatment, and allow her to focus solely on getting better while I took care of the kids. While the code dictated my actions, my love for Stef did so even more.

I didn't talk about this with my dad, my mom, my brother, my agent, or anyone. I didn't ask anyone's opinion, because I didn't want anyone to try to convince me to play (not that they could have changed my mind). The decision didn't call for some great, gallant sacrifice on my part. My love for Stef compelled me to do it, and besides, it was just the right thing to do.

For ten years, Stef had sacrificed everything for me. When I signed as a free agent with Buffalo, Green Bay and the New York Giants also made competitive offers. She and I didn't sit down to talk about the merits of each city. One day I just called her and said, "We're moving to Buffalo." I made that decision because I wanted to win a Super Bowl ring. During that decade the Bills had dominated the AFC, the American Football Conference, and they needed a middle linebacker, so Buffalo fit my agenda. I didn't consult Stef or ask her approval. Everything revolved around me and my career.

Well, now the time had come for me to make it as easy on her as possible. I just couldn't leave her in Columbus while I went off to training camp. What kind of man would I be if I deserted her when she needed me most? What kind of husband would I be if I kept on doing my own thing when she got sick? Did I want her sister holding her hand while she suffered? Did I want Stef's mom sitting with her in the hospital while they shot her full of those awful drugs? Did I want some neighbor explaining to my children why Mommy's hair fell out all over the place? No. It was my family, my responsibility, my home, and my duty.

I loved Stef more than I loved my own life. Nothing more than love compelled me to walk away from the NFL that season. If I had been granted a single wish, I would have reached into her body, pulled out the cancer, and taken it into my own to spare her this ordeal. While I couldn't do that, I could determine my response to this whole mess.

And I would not leave Stef alone at home in Columbus, or drag her to upstate New York and away from her doctors at The James.

I also knew that my kids would someday run into a difficult decision like this in their own lives. Even though Maddie was four and Noah was two, I wanted them to learn from their parents' actions, not just our words. I hoped this example would prompt them to make a similar decision if they ever faced a similar adversity. This might help instill a core foundation they could lean on. It might plant a seed that would prompt some sort of meaningful sacrifice of their own.

Stef had sacrificed for me throughout our marriage, while I concentrated on my NFL career. Now I needed to do the same for her. I knew she would try to talk me out of it. She *always* put others first. Still, I didn't expect such an emotional reaction when I walked into our bedroom and said, "I've thought about this, and it's the only way. I'm taking a year off from football to deal with this."

She was devastated. She took it harder than she did the cancer diagnosis. "You can't do this," she said, starting to cry. "You have to go. You *have* to go."

I just said, "I'm not going. I'm staying here with you. My mind's made up."

I comforted her as she rested on our bed and reassured her that nothing but my love for her motivated me to make the decision. I tried to convince her that I genuinely wanted to stay home with her and not play that season. I told her she mattered so much more to me than football, which she already knew; but I needed to make sure she understood. When our conversation ended, I went back downstairs so she could sleep, satisfied that she had grudgingly given in. Instead, she soon came back down the stairs, even more upset than before.

She cried and cried and told me, "The cancer is inside me. I don't want it affecting you. I don't want it to interrupt your career. That's what you worked your whole life for. Don't put that on me."

"You didn't do this to me," I said. "The cancer did."

She continued to protest, but I stood firm. I stressed that while all of my focus away from her and our kids had made my football career possible, she and our family always mattered the most to me. I sensed that even though she remained upset, deep down it gave her a sense of relief to know I'd be there with her all the way, no matter what happened.

I couldn't have asked for a better reaction from the Bills when I called to say I wouldn't play the 1998 season. They understood my decision and expressed their support. They didn't even make an issue about trying to regain some of the signing bonus they paid me after renegotiating my original free-agent deal to make it more salary-cap friendly after my first season there in 1996. They could have asked for some of that money back, but they didn't. They said to take whatever time I needed and to let them know when I wanted to return.

The public relations staff in Buffalo set up a press conference for me to explain my decision to the media via telephone from Columbus. Right before it started, I looked at Stef and asked, "What do you want me to tell them is the reason? Should I say it's a family issue?"

"Tell them your wife has breast cancer," she said. "Maybe that will help someone. Maybe a husband will tell his wife, 'Hey, my favorite football player's wife has breast cancer. Have you gotten a mammogram?'"

That day it became our mission to make her diagnosis public in hopes of helping others. We saw it as our calling, our divine purpose. We wouldn't have chosen this path, but now that we had to walk it, we determined to use our experience and our lives as an opportunity to serve men and women who might need our help.

So after spending the first twenty-two years of my life wanting to be a professional football player, and the last eleven years being one, I would get a new job.

I was about to become Mr. Mom.

THE BARGAIN

THE NOBLE INTENTIONS I HAD FOR MY CHILDREN LEARNING GREAT life lessons from our cancer battle soon ran smack into the reality of me doing the everyday tasks their mother had performed. The result wasn't pretty.

When I made breakfast, lunch, or dinner, I quickly learned that if any piece of food touched another piece of food, it grossed out my children. The slightest contact between two separate things on the same plate made both completely inedible to them. They also recoiled in horror at the very notion of bath time. I think Maddie and Noah thought I planned to dump them in acid, not warm water. Some kids actually enjoy a bath, but my kids preferred sleeping in their own soot and grime.

While engaged in those battles, I also struggled to keep my head above water on the laundry front. When I played, even after I first got married, I took all my laundry and put it in my mesh bag at the stadium for the equipment guys to wash. They'd yell at me, but they always did it. Now I had to sort the clothes by color and use the right temperature when I washed them. It started out ugly, but I adapted pretty fast.

I used a lot of my football lessons to figure things out. Surviving in the NFL requires learning from your mistakes. Those who continue making mistakes soon lose their job. So I educated myself and got through it. The best thing about it? I learned little nuances about my kids that I didn't know before.

Stef had spent far more time with them than I had. When training camp started in July and throughout the season, I would see the kids for only an hour or two every night before they went to bed. During the off-season, I played with them a lot and we did things together as a family. But the bond Maddie and Noah formed with Stef six months out of the year made her the person they ran to when they needed something. Now the kids depended on me for almost everything. My routine differed from Stef's, and I didn't function as smoothly. But they adjusted and we made it work.

What little free time I had when not scrambling to corral a two- and a four-year-old, I tried to use educating myself on breast cancer. I wanted to understand what we were up against. I didn't want to leave any possibility unexplored if it could help Stef feel better or get better—so I worked hard at it, just as in the NFL I studied game film for hours on end to make sure I got myself totally prepared. At first, I peppered the doctor with so many questions that he started ending every appointment the same way: "OK, Chris, what do you have for me this time?" It made me feel good to know I could ask him, "Why are we doing this? Why aren't we doing that?"

My research showed that sweets tended to hurt Stef's long-term prognosis, so I became pretty strict about what she ate. Now and then, she would sneak a piece of cake or a cookie, and I'd give her a serious look and say, "C'mon. We've gotta beat this thing." She had a sweet tooth and I felt bad for her, but I wanted to gain any edge we could, even if it was just percentage points. She took twenty vitamin supplements a day. I made sure we ate healthy as a family. I looked for anything that would help give her as much chance of winning this battle as possible. About forty of our neighbors stepped up and did a lot of the cooking for us. They did a great job following my order for foods low in fat, with no sugar, and plenty of green vegetables.

It truly inspired me to watch the determination and courage Stef showed as we moved toward her first chemo treatment. I know it scared her, but she never let on. She began journaling her feelings to cope with the stress and uncertainty she faced. That allowed her to voice some of her doubts and give herself an occasional pep talk, like she did in this entry from July:

I never thought I could love my family more than I did, but I do. I am a happy person. I really don't like being sad. I always try to find the good things in life. I know God is with me. I know there is a reason God gave me breast cancer, and I'm supposed to do something with it. Life throws us a lot of curveballs, sometimes all at once. I think God has a reason and a plan for all of it. Now is the time for me to suck it up and follow the path put before me. I'm thirty years old and I have breast cancer. My life already has had some struggles, but I have been so fortunate and blessed and truly fulfilled. I have love, excitement, thrill, and adventure. I am otherwise healthy and physically fit and have always been confident and sure of my capabilities.

I am trying to direct my strength to get me through this new chapter in my life. I will beat this thing. I have to. Madison and Noah are so much motivation. I will do anything for them. Chris, too. I need him so much, it's not even funny.

Every single emotion she felt came pouring out in that entry. Facing the unknown left us both battling fear and desperation like we'd never known. We handled the roller coaster, thanks to a lot of prayer and the strength we received from the cards and letters that filled our mailbox every day. Our friends, and a lot of people we had never met, many of them cancer survivors, strengthened us with their encouragement and inspiration. Stef and I almost raced to the mailbox to get them. As she wrote a few days before chemo started: "It's like I joined some close-knit club when I got breast cancer. I would never choose to join this club if given the choice, but I'm so grateful to the women who want to help others through it. It is motivating, inspiring, and it helps so much."

She started chemo on August 4, less than a month after her mastectomy. Her arm and chest still hurt from the surgery, and now she faced having poison pumped into her system for months in hopes of killing the cancer cells. She looked right at the needle in her arm as the Adriamycin started flowing into her veins. For forty-five minutes, she rarely took her eyes off that bright red liquid entering her body, knowing full well it would wreak havoc on her in ways she couldn't yet comprehend.

The difficulty didn't take long to arrive. That night, right before dinner, Stef began suffering an episode of the chills and started feeling queasy. I made dinner, hoping it would help her feel better. Instead, she took one look and gagged. Within an hour, after eating just a little bit of fruit salad, she threw up.

The chemotherapy treatments continued once a week for five months. I stressed to Stef that despite how lousy she felt, chemo was the good guy. Although the side effects stank, chemo was our ally. She had to take steps backward at first to take steps forward in the future. I tried, like a coach, to keep her focused on getting better and thinking positive. She bought in completely because she resolved to weather whatever it took to beat cancer and resume the life she enjoyed before her diagnosis. She tackled the chemo with everything she had, even though chemo lived up to the worst things we had heard. Stef struggled big-time with the nausea and fatigue, but never complained once.

It took an emotional toll when her hair started falling out after her second treatment. The hair loss really traumatized her. The first time she walked into a wig store, she started crying. But then, in true Stef fashion, she seized control of the situation. One day, while she wrestled on the floor with Noah, he rolled over and came up with a mouthful of her hair. Right after that, she called her hairdresser. Stef didn't want chemo to take her hair. *She* would decide how she lost her hair, so she had her head shaved. Of course, Stef made it an event. The "Hair Picnic," she called it. The kids watched and ate peanut-butter-and-jelly sandwiches on the patio while Stef sat in a chair with a handheld mirror as the hair that helped her land modeling jobs all over the country and in Greece came off in bunches.

I intended to be there and see it all happen, but I arrived a little late. I was having my own head shaved in a sign of solidarity. I wanted to divert attention away from Stef. I wanted the kids to feel comfortable with how she looked. She wouldn't seem different to them if we both looked the same. I also wanted to show that whatever came our way, it couldn't defeat us as long as we stood together. So now we sported a matched set of bald heads. Stef wore hers like a badge of courage and so did I. We were teammates, right down to the skin on our skulls.

That night, Stef told the kids we would have a hat party. She tried on different hats and wigs and so did they. I took care of playing the music and making silly commentary, like a moderator at a fashion show. We tried to send the message to our kids that cancer couldn't destroy us. We could still have fun as a family. We could still laugh. Through tears, maybe, but we could laugh. After the party, Stef told me, "That was one of the best moments we've had as a family in our entire lives."

Those good times, though, did not outnumber the difficult times. The side effects of chemo accumulated and beat Stef down. The more treatments she had, the more drugs that went into her system, the worse the nausea and fatigue and other symptoms became. The fatigue proved disheartening to someone who had run three miles a day, five days a week, before her diagnosis. As if she didn't get poked and prodded enough at The James, I injected her abdomen four times a week with Neupogen, a drug to boost her white blood cell count. I hated doing that. Because of her firm commitment and determination to do everything she could to get better, she got mad at me a few times for hesitating.

Even so, Stef struggled with depression. Her inability to join us in things we previously had done together as a family really brought her down. When I took the kids to McDonald's or Chuck E. Cheese, Stef stood at the door, crying as we drove away. She wanted to go with us, but her body wouldn't allow it. She needed to rest. She also had "chemo fog," a condition that comes over time, which left her in a daze, not thinking clearly.

For that reason, we had only one serious what-if conversation about the future. She sat at the kitchen table one morning, feeling sick, while the kids ate breakfast and played with their toys. They paid no attention to us while we engaged in a very frank conversation, right there in front of them, about what might happen if Stef died. We had never really talked about that possibility before, but for some reason, we started talking about it that morning. Something seemed very natural about that. It was the most important conversation we ever had, and we had it over coffee while the kids ate their cereal. Stef and I could always talk to each other like that. I loved how I could be direct with her and she could be direct with me, and neither of us ever felt hurt when the other just said what they were thinking.

She didn't hold anything back that morning, but I kept one thing hidden from her. I think most men have a natural instinct to protect their wives and children. Because of that, I blamed myself for letting this thing—this threat to my wife's life and our happy existence as a family—into our lives. I knew that made no sense, but I couldn't stop thinking that I, as a husband and father, had allowed cancer into my house to threaten my wife and my children's mother.

My football background had ingrained in me that, no matter what I faced, I could out-tough it, out-physical it, or out-hit it. But finally I faced an opponent I couldn't control. It wasn't even a fair fight. I had no opportunity to compete on even terms with cancer, and I really struggled with that. My Christian walk lacked maturity back then and I focused on all my past sins. A twisted logic caused me to ask, "What did I do to bring this on us?" I knew better than to think of Stef's cancer as some sort of punishment, but sometimes my mind just ran wild, and those crazy thoughts occasionally took over. So while Stef had her battle with chemo, I struggled with misplaced guilt.

Looking back, I realize I also really struggled with submitting to God's authority. I didn't rebel and shake my fist at the heavens—far from it! I ran to God for comfort—but I still didn't submit. Instead, I tried to bargain with Him. I had conversations with Him late at night, long after everyone else in the house had fallen asleep. I would watch infomercials on TV just to kill time. Occasionally I would talk to God out loud about whatever came to mind.

One night, as I watched the Alien Wedge infomercial, I turned from my chair toward the couch after the guy in the infomercial hit a golf ball off the bed of a dump truck. "Hey, Jesus," I said, "I don't think You can hit that shot." Then I laughed and I imagined Him laughing too. "Yeah, I think I can," I imagined Him saying. "OK," I said, "I have a deal for You. You get me through this, and I'll take care of everything else. We'll call it even." By that I meant, "Heal Stef and I won't bother You with any minor crap."

Obviously, that approach fell far short of submitting to God and whatever He planned for our lives. I still thought, or hoped, I had *some* control over what remained ahead of us. Of course, I didn't have any control, which became very clear to me over time.

Skipping the 1998 season to care for Stef took me away from playing organized football for the first time since I became eligible to play Midget League when I turned nine years old. Most people who knew me figured I would flip out because I had the reputation — among those in the NFL and outside the league — of someone completely consumed with football. I earned that reputation because I cultivated exactly that image with how little I allowed people to see of me away from the game.

Although I loved my wife and family more than anything else, until the possibility of cancer taking Stef away from us hit me squarely in the face, football was my god. I'm ashamed to admit that, but I can't deny it. I received letters from teammates when I announced I wouldn't play in 1998. Most of them said how much it surprised them that I would give up football for *anything*. I rarely gave anyone the impression that anything else mattered more to me.

In fact, though, I didn't struggle as much with not playing as I did with the idea that I was no longer a football player. I had played football my entire adult life, so I had no other identity. Sitting out the last half of the previous season with my neck injury made it easier, but still not easy, to realize, *Hey, this phase of my life may be over.*

No matter how willingly I'd decided to sit out in 1998, at times I still felt conflicted. Sure, I wanted to be with Stef; but on game days I also really missed playing. It might not have bothered me quite so much if I had just removed myself from the game as much as possible, but I didn't do that. Instead, I bought extra TVs. I had one in the basement, one in the bedroom, one in the kitchen, one in the family room, and one in my weight room. On Sunday afternoons, I turned on every TV and walked around the house from room to room, watching the NFL. I grew so frustrated watching one game and not being able to play, that I'd walk into another room, where I'd see a different game. I did that from 1 p.m. to 7 p.m. every week. Why didn't I just turn the games off? I don't know. It captivated me, like a car wreck pulled off to the side of the road. I just *had* to watch it.

The Bills started 0–3, which made it even tougher. Whenever you sit out in football, it's miserable, whether your team wins or loses. If it wins, you think, *They must not need me.* If the team loses, you feel guilty and think, *It would be different if I could play.* I didn't have much contact with the Bills except for one visit to Buffalo. I drove up on a Sunday morning. I talked to a few guys in the locker room before their game against the 49ers. After kickoff, they introduced me over the loud speaker and the fans gave me a standing ovation.

I loved playing in Buffalo. Bills' fans really appreciated an honest effort. I'd been there only a year and a half, but they knew I'd given them everything I had. Still, watching from the sidelines that day really stank. I hated it.

For a decade I had defined myself as an NFL player and for ten years before that I did nothing but dream about it. So it felt almost surreal to be watching—but unable to participate in—something that had been a part of my life *forever*. And it went on just fine without me.

Later that fall, Stef and I visited Cincinnati to see her sister Sue and her family. I first met Sue when I attended her wedding with Stef, who was sixteen at the time. I wore my brother's too-tight sports coat and a pair of borrowed dress shoes, and I *really* felt out of my comfort zone. But I wanted to support Stef, meet her extended family, and wish Sue well, so even though I was an extremely shy, introverted kid who found that kind of social interaction very hard, I bucked up. I acted like I thought a man should act—better, in fact, than I acted during this trip to Cincinnati. I happened to be watching TV when an NFL commercial came on. I stuck my fingers in my ears and started singing, "Na-Na-Nah-Na-Na-Nah," like a little kid who doesn't want to hear it's time to go to bed. I consoled myself with the knowledge that the extra time away would give my neck another year to heal. When the 1998 season ended and I could start looking forward to playing again in 1999, it felt like someone had lifted a giant weight off my chest.

The Bills eventually made the playoffs without me, but lost in the first round on Saturday, January 2. Stef had her last chemo on Tuesday, January 5. We had looked forward to that day for so long that we wanted to celebrate. Now that it had finally arrived, we planned a trip to Disney World with the kids. One day at the park, as we waited for the Dumbo Ride, Stef smiled at me and said, "You know what? I haven't thought about cancer all day."

CHAPTER 4

THE COMEBACK

THE END OF STEF'S CHEMOTHERAPY AND CLEAN BILL OF HEALTH allowed her to resume more of a normal life. It allowed me to focus more fully on my return to the NFL.

Throughout her treatment, I snuck away whenever I could and worked out at Ohio State, dialing in on the kind of condition I would need to reclaim my spot in Buffalo. Not wanting to waste a single day in my preparations, I'd wait for Stef and the kids to go to bed at Disney World, then I'd go down to the first floor of our hotel, the Fort Wilderness Resort. Families straggling in from a day at the park gave me some pretty funny looks as I went through my linebacker drills in the lobby.

John Holecek, a young guy from the University of Illinois, played my position for the Bills while I sat out. I liked John. I knew he had a good career ahead of him, but I had every intention of reclaiming my spot in the lineup. I went to mini-camp hoping to prove to the coaches that they could count on me, but I lacked medical clearance to participate in any contact, so I couldn't make the impression I wanted.

I returned home to Columbus and continued to work out. A few weeks later, in February, the Bills called and asked me to come up and meet with John Butler, the general manager; Wade Phillips, the head coach; and Ted Cottrell, the defensive coordinator. I drove to Buffalo, sat down with all three, and listened while they told me where I stood. I didn't like what I heard.

They wanted me to serve as Holecek's mentor, kind of a player/coach. They planned on me splitting time with him to see how that worked, which did not appeal to me at all. I told them I appreciated

45

everything they had done for me, but if they preferred to go in that direction, I wanted them to release me or trade me. I had zero interest in anything short of coming back and picking up where I left off—as the starter and the guy who called our defense on the field. I believed I could still play at a Pro Bowl level, like I did up to the midpoint of the 1997 season when I broke my neck. I understood their situation. They had a young player who didn't cost them as much money, who they felt replaced me pretty effectively while I couldn't play. I didn't need any time to think about my reaction. I didn't get mad, but I had absolutely no interest in backing up anyone. We parted on good terms. I gave John, Wade, and Ted each a hug and drove back to Upper Arlington, the suburb in Columbus where we lived.

Before long, John Butler contacted the Cleveland Browns, an expansion team about to come back into existence after a three-year absence following the original Browns' move to Baltimore. John asked if the Browns had any interest in me. They had enough curiosity to ask me to come to Cleveland for a workout. The Bills still owned my rights, so they didn't have to allow that, but they did. I met with Chris Palmer, the Browns' coach; Carmen Policy, part of the ownership group; and Dwight Clark, the general manager. I took a physical at the Cleveland Clinic. A day or two later, Buffalo traded me to Cleveland for "past considerations." Basically, Buffalo gave me away for nothing. The Browns hadn't existed since moving to Baltimore in 1996, so Buffalo certainly didn't owe Cleveland anything for "past considerations." John Butler did me a huge favor by trading me back home. He didn't have to do that, but the teams I played for always treated me well and never screwed me over, like happens to some players. I'll be forever grateful for that. I hope I earned that with the way I played and with my production.

Even though, as an expansion franchise, the Browns had no real hope of winning a Super Bowl, I liked a lot of things about landing in Cleveland. Its proximity to Columbus, just 140 miles away, allowed Stef and the kids to stay at home during the season. She could keep her same set of doctors at Ohio State. Second, I got caught up in the excitement that everyone in northeast Ohio felt over the Browns returning to the NFL. Cleveland felt like the perfect place for me to finish my career, just an hour from where I played in high school in Massillon. And, as a bonus, we would play our first exhibition in the Pro Football Hall of Fame game in Canton, where I grew up.

The question of whether my neck could withstand the punishment of an entire NFL season caused the Browns to insist I sign a waiver in my contract. If I hurt my neck, they would owe me nothing. In exchange for that, I negotiated a workout bonus. They wanted me there in the off season to establish a work ethic for the younger guys and help bring them along. I liked that idea. I thought it would be cool at the end of my career to help build something from the ground up.

I settled into a routine that started over every Sunday night, when I drove to Cleveland. I worked out with the team on Monday, stayed the night, and then drove home after Tuesday workouts. We had Wednesdays off, so I spent that day at home in Upper Arlington with the family. Thursday morning, I drove back to Cleveland for workouts, stayed that night in a hotel, and then drove back home after Friday workouts. I spent the weekends at home. That's how I planned to do it throughout the season so Stef and the kids wouldn't suffer too much disruption in their lives.

I couldn't wait to get back to the NFL. I figured my neck fusion would work just fine. I hadn't played in an NFL game since week eight of the 1997 season, almost two years earlier. Since my surgery that fall, I had worked out with Dave Kennedy, the strength coach for the football program at Ohio State. Dave didn't just put me through lifting and football drills. He became a very close friend and someone I trusted. Dave was the first person I told about Stef's breast cancer after her initial diagnosis in July 1998. I shared my worst fears with him, and only him. I felt very comfortable confiding in Dave, not just my football worries, but my at-home worries. I think we clicked because he approached everything from an athlete's perspective, like I did. He didn't give me platitudes about my situation or Stef's. He dealt in reality. Whenever I told Dave bad news about Stef's diagnosis or treatment, he would say something like, "Put another rock in that backpack you're carrying and keep climbing the mountain."

Most people in that situation don't know what to say, so they say what they think you want to hear. It did me no good to hear someone say, "Don't worry, Chris. Everything will turn out fine." How would they know? No one could guarantee it, so why say it? I think it takes a strong person to admit, "Hey, there are no guarantees." Dave took that approach. His personality meshed well with mine. I wanted to attack my training to give myself the best chance for success. I believed strongly in doing everything I could to position myself for a successful comeback. Dave drove me toward that goal without promising me anything. He didn't give me any false hope. I respected him for that, and our friendship grew.

I built up a tremendous amount of anticipation for my first game back. My dad's teams at Canton Timken played their home games in Fawcett Stadium, and I played there twice in the Massillon-McKinley games during my high school career. Now things had come full circle for me, winding up in Cleveland and in Canton as my career neared the end.

I wondered if my instincts would still be there after sitting out a year and a half. But after the first play in training camp, I knew I'd be fine. It felt like I'd never left the game. But then, early in camp, I hit one of our fullbacks, Tarek Saleh, and that old feeling of momentary paralysis overtook me. It didn't knock me to my knees, but I had a hard time feeling my wobbly legs. That made me so angry. I thought the neck fusion had fixed the problem. I thought I'd done enough hitting to eliminate the possibility of it happening again. I'd hit Tarek pretty hard and the paralysis disappeared pretty quickly, so I decided to ignore it. I told myself, "I'm fine. It's nothing." I continued to practice that day and the rest of that week leading up to the Hall of Fame game. I played OK that night in front of a bunch of old friends and family. It felt good to get back in the groove again.

We played Minnesota in our second exhibition game, Tampa Bay in our third, and Chicago to wrap up the preseason at home. The coaches didn't plan on playing me long against the Bears, because most teams rest their veterans the final week of the preseason to have them ready when the real games start the following week. I expected to come out after the first quarter, but I didn't last even that long before it happened again.

I dropped into the flat, defending against a screen pass, when Chicago's center, Casey Wiegmann, blindsided me. I didn't see him coming because I had my eyes on the back coming out of the backfield. Casey gave me a pretty good shot and I went down. Lying there, looking up at the stars, I was completely paralyzed. For some reason it didn't scare me. I thought about Stef, Maddie, and Noah watching the game at home in Upper Arlington. I knew they would be freaking out. Maddie knew I had neck issues. She asked me once before I left for training camp, "Daddy, if you're in a wheelchair, does that mean we can't go swimming anymore?"

The trainers came onto the field, which I hated. I knew they were just doing their job, but in my entire career I'd never gone down long enough with an injury that any trainer had to come out and check on me. As I lay there, I heard them say they wanted to bring out a stretcher. My pride didn't want that to happen. I started getting some tingling in my arms and legs, so I recognized this as just another episode like the others, only a little worse. Still, they helped me to the sidelines, which really ticked me off. I'd made an oath—a stupid oath, but a part of my code—that if I ever needed help off the field, I'd better be dead or else I would be done.

Right then, I knew my career was over.

The trainers took me into the locker room and rushed me to the Cleveland Clinic for an MRI. It showed that the neck fusion designed to fix my injury two years earlier had held up just fine, but I had another disc causing this current problem. It had degenerated and stuck out, leaving very little room between that disc and my spinal cord. When the bad disc brushed against my cord, it caused bouts of temporary paralysis. The more I brushed the cord, the greater the chance I would suffer one catastrophic event in which I would never regain feeling in my arms and legs. Once I heard that, I came clean with the doctors about my earlier episode of paralysis in practice a few weeks earlier. That confirmed their diagnosis.

As soon as I could, I called Stef from the Cleveland Clinic and told her not to worry. I assured her that I could walk and that I felt fine. "I need you to come to Cleveland tomorrow morning." She asked why, and I told her, "Because this is it. I can't play anymore."

As fanatically as I had approached my comeback, and despite my ability to play through pain and injuries, I knew I had to stop. I couldn't perform like I needed to, and I didn't want to become the kind of player I despised—afraid to hit someone because I might get paralyzed. I remember thinking, *I'm glad an injury took me out of the game*. There's a chance I could have become one of those guys who hang on and on and on. But now, I had no options. I had no choice. My neck made the choice for me that Saturday night, August 28, 1999.

Stef came to Cleveland and accompanied me to my press conference. Before it started, I told my teammates I had to leave the game. I purposely avoided using the word "retire." I preferred a different label than "retirement." I said my injuries forced me to walk away from the game. "I would love to keep playing," I said at the press conference, "but I can't jeopardize my legs and my arms. It's difficult to say, 'No more.' It's hard. But I don't have any regrets. I wish I could still be playing, but that's not possible. I've been very fortunate to be an NFL player. That's the hard part. To wake up tomorrow morning and know I'm not an NFL player anymore."

Just before my senior year at Ohio State, the *Columbus Dispatch* did a Sunday magazine story about me in which my mom spoke about how I would handle a career-ending injury: "Our fear is not so much an injury; it's how he will deal with it if it happens," she told them. "The thing I (worry) about at times is when he can't play anymore or if he gets injured and can't play."

I understand why she felt that way, but my attitude and understanding had changed over the years. Stef's cancer diagnosis, her chemo treatments, and spending that year with our children during her recovery gave me a different perspective. Compared to the scare I had with Stef's diagnosis—which forced me to consider the possibility of life without her—the end of my football career seemed small and insignificant. I always knew football would end someday.

But until Stef's diagnosis, I never considered something that serious would occur with *her* health.

Of course, if given the choice, I would have preferred to remain an NFL player. Not playing for a year while taking care of Stef eased my acceptance of transitioning into life without the sport. I absorbed the initial shock because I already had dealt with some of those feelings after my injury and during Stef's chemo. Still, as we drove back to Columbus that Sunday, I approached the rest of my life as a thirty-three-year-old guy with a wife, two children, and no earthly idea what I would do with my time.

That made me uneasy, but for the first time I realized the blessing of facing such a dilemma. My eleven years in the NFL had left us in a great situation financially. I'm sure many cancer husbands would love to stay home with their wives during chemotherapy. Very few can, because very few can afford it. I stressed that fact to everyone who tried to suggest I had sacrificed a lot by skipping the 1998 season. I'm sure any husband would do the same thing if they didn't have to go to work every day to earn a living.

I knew that eventually I would find some sort of a job, although I had no clear idea what that might be. Most people confront indecision about their career long before their early thirties. Some can't decide what profession they want to pursue after graduating from high school or college. Some discover they don't like their chosen field once they've worked in it for a while. But me? I loved everything about being an NFL player. As early as I could remember, and for every minute of my childhood and teenage years, I had put every single ounce of energy and preparation into achieving that dream. God had created me with a unique drive, ability to focus, and single-minded vision that, in my early years, I channeled almost exclusively into football. On the playing field I received most of my early training and preparation for the great challenges Stef and I would face in the future; and although I let the game consume me more than I should have, yet God used even my youthful addiction to football to equip me for much bigger things in years to come.

CHAPTER 5

GROWING UP

BEFORE MY FATHER RAISED ME TO BE A LINEBACKER, HE RAISED ME
to be something else.

A hunting dog.

He dressed me up in old football uniforms with whatever pads
he could scrounge from the teams he coached, put a helmet on me,
and out the door we'd go. My dad had a shotgun and so did my older
brother, Rick. They took me along to root through the briar bushes
and kick out the rabbits.

If anyone tried such a thing today, the authorities would grab the
children and put them in foster care. But in Canton, Ohio, as the
1960s turned into the 1970s, times were different.

And my dad, Charles "Sonny" Spielman, definitely came from a
different era.

He grew up in Canton in the 1940s and lived downtown, on the
second floor, above a confectionary store. That sounds like a great life,
a kid growing up over the top of a candy store—but my dad's father
died when my dad was twelve.

He named me Charles Christopher Spielman after the grandfather
I never met.

I think losing his father at such a young age affected my dad's
perspective on parenthood. While he coached with a lot of guys, and
probably had plenty of chances to spend nights out with his buddies,
my dad always spent whatever time he had away from coaching with
Rick and me.

He treated us as more than sons. We were his best friends, and he was our best friend. It used to drive me crazy as a toddler when Dad and Rick would leave the house without me. They told me they were going to work, but I saw through that lie. They were going to football practice. Finally I raised such a stink that they took me with them, and I became a regular in the locker room by the time I turned four.

My dad didn't plan on playing college football. He came from a family without the means for a college education, so he went to work after his high school graduation. One day, a guy with a Southern accent came to town, looking for big kids in search of a ticket out of town. Someone must have told him about my dad, who worked on a ditch-digging crew when the guy first approached him.

"Which one of you is Sonny Spielman?" he asked.

"I am," my dad answered.

"Son, how would you like to get out of that ditch and play some football?"

My dad got out that second and, after hitchhiking to Meridian, Mississippi, found himself playing football at East Mississippi State Junior College. After two years there, he moved on to St. Joseph's College in Rensselaer, Indiana. He got his teaching degree and returned to his hometown to teach at his alma mater, Canton Central Catholic.

He met my mom, Nancy, once he returned to town. They got married in 1962.

My dad became the head football coach at Canton Timken High School in 1970, when I was five years old. Once school let out for the day, Rick and I went straight to either Timken's practice or its game. In the winter, when my dad officiated high school basketball, I'd go with him, and he'd toss me the ball during timeouts so I could go out on the floor and shoot. That never made me the least bit nervous. I figured, *I'm going to show these people what I can do.* But nowhere did I desire to show people what I could do more than on the football field.

My dad's coaching career exposed me to the sport as I grew up. Most of my earliest memories involve football. Something about the game —really, *everything* about it—fascinated me. The sights, the sounds, the smells, the mouth guards, the helmets, the uniforms, the camaraderie, the contact ... I connected with all of it. For whatever reason, I found something that absolutely captivated me, something I became so passionate about at an extremely young age that I never cared about anything else. I couldn't wait to get on the field to play my first organized game.

Unfortunately, I *had* to wait. And wait. And wait some more. In Canton, boys couldn't participate in what they called Local Midget Football until they were nine years old, so Rick got a three-year head start on me. The first time he came home with his uniform, he stood on my parents' bed and admired himself in the mirror. I went crazy, running through the house, slamming doors, and shouting, "I want to play! I want to play! I can't wait three years! I've got to play!"

Since I couldn't play organized football, I resolved to work as hard as I could to get ready for when my time finally did come. I obsessed with preparing myself, down to the smallest detail. Linebackers needed quickness. So to work on my quickness, I'd take hot dogs from our refrigerator and go over to the neighbor's house. I'd show the hot dogs to their dog to get him all excited, then I'd shove the hot dogs into my pocket and try to run away from him while he chased me around their yard.

Whatever I did, it revolved around football. I had these action figures, Big Jim and Big Jack, whom I turned into football players. One time one of the arms fell off and I started crying. "My player is hurt. My player is hurt." My dad came in and said, "I'll fix him up, son." He grabbed some tape, taped his arm back on, and said, "There, he's good to play now."

At the time, we lived in a bungalow in Canton. I would run from the kitchen into the bedroom, dodging the couch and the coffee table and other imaginary defenders in my path. I'd do spin moves, hurdles, dives, always imitating guys I'd see on NFL Films highlights, Ohio State highlights, Notre Dame highlights, or the Youngstown State Penguins. Three times I had to go to the hospital after running into walls, hitting furniture, or getting tripped up. One night I fell and cut my ear. My dad took me into the bathroom and poured some rubbing alcohol on it. I asked him, "Are we going to the hospital again, Dad?"

"Yep, we're going to the hospital again, buddy."

We went, I got stitched up, and we returned home.

I had a competitive streak to match my overwhelming desire to play in the NFL. I ruined an electric football game Rick and I received for Christmas one year because the players made me mad. They wouldn't go where I wanted them to, so I smashed it.

My dad didn't allow his players much leeway on discipline. Most of his guys had no interest in going to college. They came to Timken, a vocational school, from broken homes or the poor side of town. He even had one player who the police let out of jail on Friday nights so he could play. I loved those teams because the players' difficult backgrounds made them extremely tough. My dad didn't put up with any crap from any of them. If they screwed up, he chewed them out royally. But they also knew he cared about them. A lot of those guys didn't have anything, so he'd have them over in the summer to paint our house so he could give them a few bucks, even though it didn't need painting. Even though we didn't have much growing up, Mom and Dad both always looked to give what they had, to give people some opportunity. Not just through their words, but much more through their actions, they instilled in me a deep commitment to serve others.

Timken had some talented guys, and Roddell Jackson was my favorite. Man, could he play. One night my dad, who coached from the press box and called all the offensive plays, called a reverse in the first half; Roddell scored a touchdown. As we walked back out to play the second half, I said, "Dad, run the fake reverse. They'll jump all over it. Run the fake reverse." Well, sure enough, he called a fake reverse in the second half, and Timken scored a touchdown. I stood on the sidelines, going crazy. I looked up into the press box and waved at him, like, "Hey, Dad, my play worked!" He just gave me a dismissive wave. I guess he didn't want my head to swell.

My father required effort from his players and from me. He never got on me if I failed, but if he felt I didn't try, didn't listen, or didn't play the right way, he could get very demanding. That became clear when, as a fourth grader, I fouled out of a basketball game in the first half. We had only five guys on our team that day. I guess my football mentality took over, because I kept getting called for reaching in to steal the ball. When I got my fourth foul, my dad came down from the stands and told me, "Whatever you do, don't reach in. Don't foul." Sure enough, a guy dribbled down, I reached in, and they called me for my fifth foul. I didn't have to find my dad in the crowd to hear his reaction: "DUMB! DUMB ASS! YOU'RE WALKING HOME!" So I walked home. Normally he gave me positive reinforcement and I had his approval most of the time. But in that instance, I learned an important lesson about team. His way of teaching that lesson didn't come from a book written by a well-respected therapist. It came in hit-me-over-the-head-with-a-hammer fashion. I had a three-mile walk home, learning the lesson: "Your teammates are counting on you. Don't foul out." Those early lessons about teamwork had a profound effect on me years later when Stef and I found ourselves in the middle of our battle against cancer.

Both my dad and mom did a great job keeping Rick and me grounded while showing us lots of love. They never pushed us into anything, but they supported us completely in whatever we did. We got constant encouragement from my mom. She did everything for us. The competitiveness between Rick and me really bothered her. We'd go at it sometimes, and she'd say, "Sonny, make them stop!" He'd just say, "Oh, they're all right." Sometimes he would even egg Rick on by saying, "Hey, you're not going to let your little brother get away with that, are you?" Boy, whenever he said that, the battle really heated up.

My parents also did a great job giving us a realistic perspective on life. We didn't have a lot, since my dad made about $22,000 a year by teaching and then working in the summers at the Canton Jewish Community Center. But whatever we had, we shared with others. One Christmas Eve, my dad took Rick and me to the downtown YMCA, where we picked up one of his Timken players, Harry Brown, who lived there. Harry came over to our house and spent Christmas with us the next day. My mom had presents for him. She and my dad treated him like one of the family. It made a huge impression on me to realize that I had so many things that some eighteen-year-old kids lacked. When we dropped Harry off at the YMCA that night, we visited his room. You could just about spread your arms out and touch both walls. He didn't even have a TV.

On the way home I said, "Dad, why does he live there?"

My dad replied, "Because he doesn't have anywhere else to go, son."

When it came to playing football, I grew to prize the same quality my father loved the most—toughness. For that reason, I loved playing against older kids. It gave me a way to become tougher. It challenged me far more than playing with kids my own age. One time, while playing with Rick and some of his friends in a sandlot game at Lehman Junior High School, I hit a kid who ran the ball in my direction. I hit him so hard, he quit right there, on the spot. "I'm not playing with him anymore," he said, pointing at me. I took pride in knowing I had made someone quit. I knew then I had something that made me different from other kids my age.

At Edgefield Elementary School, I got detention only once—for lying to the playground monitor about playing tag. Instead, we had been playing tackle football, which the school didn't allow. I considered the rule stupid, so I started recruiting spies among the kids who didn't want to play. I told them to watch the monitor and warn me so we wouldn't get caught. That worked pretty well and kept me out of trouble.

When I finally turned nine and could play organized tackle football, I had a problem. I weighed ninety-four pounds, and they established the weight limit for a running back at ninety pounds. So I started training to drop the weight. I jogged from our home on Thirty-Sixth Street, across a path in an adjacent field over to Thirty-Seventh Street, up the hill, down to Cleveland Avenue, and then back home. I did that for a solid week, four laps a day, with plastic bags on my legs and arms. At the weigh-in, I came in at 87 pounds—under the limit and ready to make my mark.

It didn't take long for me to understand that I had more ability than other kids. I scored three touchdowns and intercepted a pass in my first game, playing running back and linebacker. My dad pointed out the good things and the bad things I did, and he said something afterward I remember to this day: "Son, I see you doing things I can't get my high school players to do." I took that as a sign that I had a chance to realize my dream of playing in the NFL.

Of course, I had an advantage, given my upbringing and thirst for the game. I began going to two-a-day practices at Timken by the time I turned four. When I was six or seven, instead of wrestling around with Rick on the sidelines, my dad sent me elsewhere. "Go watch Bernie Hall," he'd say. "He coaches linebackers. That's what you are." So I'd watched Bernie Hall coach linebackers. I'd sit in their meetings. I understood the difference between a cover-two and a cover-three defense. I learned gap responsibilities. I didn't know it at the time, but I was being shaped and molded.

Don't take that to mean I objected in any way or that it went against my will. I *loved* it. I craved it. I enjoyed being there. The desire to drink in everything about football came from within me. My dad didn't force anything on me, but he didn't discourage it either. He whet my obsession just by saying the things football coaches say, like, "You've got to be able to bend your knees to be a good player." So whenever I went down the hall to the bathroom or from our bedroom to the kitchen, I'd waddle or duck walk, like Groucho Marx. I hung on my dad's every word about football because he coached the sport.

When he told me Alan Page of the Minnesota Vikings came from Canton Central Catholic, I became a Vikings fan. I loved the Purple People Eaters and the rest of the Vikings, like Chuck Foreman and Sammy White, Jeff Wright, Bobby Brown, Paul Krause, Ron Yary, Ed Marinaro, and on and on. Not many seven-year-olds could name the entire starting lineup of the Minnesota Vikings, but I could. I had an uncommon attention span — but only for football, not for anything else. Everything else bored me.

I suppose a psychologist would say that didn't make me a very well-rounded kid. I played every sport possible, but football always ranked first on my priority list. Was I single-minded? Absolutely. I'm proud of that. It helped me reach my goals. God put that single-mindedness in me, not merely to play football, but to give me the tools I would need later on to face challenges much, much bigger than football. And I think He does similar things for all of us.

My competitive streak, of course, applied to a lot more than football. One Monday when we didn't have school, I went to the Jewish Community Center to play basketball. The gym opened at 8 a.m., and I didn't return home until nine that night. I stopped shooting and playing only once—to go to the bathroom. I didn't stop to eat or get a drink. I was having too much fun to stop. But I also thought, *I wonder if any other fifth or sixth grader is doing what I'm doing? I wonder if there's a record for shooting baskets the longest?* We had a basketball hoop at home, and before I came in the house, I would say, "OK, if I make six out of ten, I'll play Division I football. If I make ten out of ten, I'll play in the NFL." Of course, I wouldn't go in the house until I made ten out of ten. Even that young, whatever I did, I graded it against the scale of what it would take to play professional football.

Another time, I went to the Edgewood Swimming Club as a guest. I went with my mom and my aunt and some cousins. That afternoon we planned to go to Cedar Point, an amusement park about an hour away. But then I saw this kid doing a one and a half off the high dive. Once I saw that, I refused to leave until I learned how to do it. I failed miserably on my first six or seven tries, smacking my back or my face on the surface of the water. The people around the pool probably wondered, *What is he doing?* My aunt tried to hurry me along, but my mom said, "You're not going to change his mind, so just leave him alone." About the seventh or eighth time, the kid who had done the dive came up to me and said, "You gotta spin faster." So then I nailed one. My aunt said, "OK, you did it, let's go. If we don't leave now, we're going to screw up the whole day." I answered, "I'm not leaving until I do ten." I always tested myself that way. So I did ten. Then we went to Cedar Point.

Before I started fifth grade, we moved from the Glen Oak school district three miles down the road into the Canton city school district. My dad wanted us to be there, perhaps for cultural reasons. I know this: the first day of school that fall, I heard kids saying things in everyday conversation that I'd heard previously only in locker rooms. I didn't mind the move because the city league established the weight limit for running backs and quarterbacks at 110 pounds. That excited me. These were bigger kids, tougher kids, and better athletes. I played quarterback, running back, and linebacker and loved every minute of it.

Some parents of other kids in the league didn't like me. They circulated a petition to get me banned because I hit a kid and broke his arm. I was big and I hit hard. That bothered some people. I never tried to hurt anyone, but I also never felt bad about hurting someone. I believed in going all out, all the time. Injuries just happen. They're part of the game. Parents would shout things at me and yell at their own kids, "Break his legs," and things like that. That just excited me more and made me play harder. Many times, my dad stood off to the side or in the end zone, a long distance away, so he wouldn't hear what people yelled at me. That way, he didn't get into any fights.

Since they couldn't get me banned from the league, they tried to make a rule that linebackers had to weigh less than 130 pounds. By now, at twelve years old, I weighed 145 pounds. Under no circumstances could I get down to 130, so I just outsmarted them. I'd line up four yards off the ball at nose guard, then, right before they snapped the ball, I'd stand up and play linebacker.

When I got to Lehman Junior High, a levy failure forced the district to cut all seventh-grade sports, so I had to wait until the next fall to play again. The last game of that year, we waited out a delay while some thunderstorms came through. It kept raining really, really hard. Finally, the coach came in and told us they canceled the game. I just went off. "What do you mean 'canceled'? This is football! You don't cancel a game because of rain. We're supposed to play! We're supposed to play outside. It's not fair. It's not fair!" I kept on whining like someone had stolen my puppy.

The coach looked at me and said, "Relax, Chris. What are you, insane?"

I asked him, "OK, when is the makeup game? Are we playing tomorrow? The day after that? When?" I couldn't stop crying. The tears kept flowing. It made me so angry.

I *loved* the game. I loved to play. I know I was not normal in that regard. I loved it so much, in fact, that it came close to a scary level.

CHAPTER 6

WHO IS THAT GIRL?

THERE WERE NO SECRETS IN STARK COUNTY HIGH SCHOOL FOOTball. Fans in every district identified the kids in the midget league and junior high ranks who might make a difference to their team's success. I had a reputation as a potential impact player. People wondered, but didn't know, whether I'd choose to play for my father at Timken High School or play at the other school in town, McKinley.

That decision took me about two seconds. I wanted to play for the best team I could, and McKinley, a perennial powerhouse, fit that description. My dad knew I wanted to attend McKinley and he had no problem with it. McKinley evidently wanted to remove all doubt because in 1979, after his tenth year at Timken, the school made overtures to my dad about becoming the McKinley athletic director. I don't know what exactly happened, but that job never materialized.

Washington High School, in the adjacent town of Massillon, saw an opportunity to grab a good coach and—what a coincidence—two pretty good players in Rick and me. So the summer between my eighth grade and freshman year, my dad took a job as an assistant coach at Massillon, and we moved ten miles west into a town filled with people who shared my obsession with football.

Massillon bills itself as the City of Champions. The Massillon Tigers are among the most storied high school programs in the United States, having won nine mythical national championships, more than any other school in the country. Massillon's football alumni include Harry Stuhldreher, one of the famed Four Horsemen; Earle Bruce and Don James, two college football Hall of Fame coaches; twenty-three

NFL players; fourteen collegiate All-Americans; and three NFL head coaches.

Tiger football isn't among Massillon's top priorities. It is *the* top priority, and no one there apologizes for it. A live tiger cub, Obie, prowls the sidelines at every game. On Fridays, everyone in the city wears their Massillon gear. The businesses cover themselves in orange-and-black signs and streamers.

Massillon and McKinley played for the first time in 1894, and they've been arch rivals ever since. The last game of the regular season, Massillon and McKinley always play each other. They made a full-length movie—*Go Tigers*—that followed the players for an entire year just to show their singular focus on the Massillon-McKinley game. Years ago, it became the first high school football game in America to have odds listed in Las Vegas.

The second we moved to Massillon, I knew I belonged there. Not everyone shared that opinion, though. When our family moved from the Canton district into the Massillon district, alarms went off with McKinley fans. Maybe if we had moved to Marlington, Fairless, Canton South, or some other nearby school district, it wouldn't have raised such a fuss. But we had moved to join the enemy in Massillon. People couldn't do anything to stop it because my dad had a job in Massillon. But that didn't keep the McKinley fans from alleging that something dirty had gone on under the table.

That fall I entered the ninth grade at Longfellow Junior High School with one mission: I wanted to show those Massillon boys how to play football. I knew they had some tough kids and good players, but I came in with the idea of hitting anything that moved to make sure I earned their respect. We won every game that season with me playing linebacker and running back, so my reputation grew.

At the end of the season, the town's two junior high schools—Longfellow and Loren Andrews—combined teams and practiced for a week. That team then faced the Massillon High School sophomore team to give everyone a glimpse of what the future might look like.

I knew the varsity head coach, Mike Currence, would be watching our game against the sophomores, and I didn't want to waste the chance to impress him. I played my best game ever. Afterward, I watched the film with my dad. We'd watched hours and hours of film from his teams' games over the years, but I'd never seen myself play. It was so cool to watch. I must have replayed it a hundred times.

Right then, I realized the huge benefits of studying film. It helped me see the game better and understand how all the pieces fit. I felt like one of those math whizzes, someone who could see a problem and then visualize the solution. For me, on offense and defense, I could sense how things worked before the center snapped the ball. The alignment of the players gave me a clue about whether the offense or the defense would have an advantage on that play. I didn't see the game like a fan watching it. I saw beyond what appeared on the surface.

All of that, I hoped, would help me earn a starting job on the Massillon varsity in the fall. To do that, I would have to violate a very orderly progression within the Massillon High School program. Typically, guys moved from the sophomore team to the jayvee and then up to the varsity as seniors. Not many juniors could make the varsity, and even fewer of those juniors started. I had the goal not only of starting at Massillon as a junior, but to start as a sophomore. That didn't happen often, if ever.

The mere fact that I loomed as a threat to make Massillon's starting lineup as a sophomore didn't endear me to my new teammates. I had no standing with those guys, and they let me know it. I got challenged to fights, and one guy urinated on the stuff in my locker. I refused to fight my teammates; I saw no purpose in it. I just kept my head down, tried to ignore the less-than-friendly treatment, and let my actions speak. I understood why some of those guys didn't like me. I wasn't born in Massillon. I didn't get the football in my crib, given to every newborn boy in town. They saw me as a move-in, an outsider.

None of that crap mattered once we started playing. I started the opener against Massillon Perry, had an interception, and made every tackle on the kickoff team. A couple of weeks later, we played Cincinnati Moeller — a six-time state champion — and I had a big game. I knew then, playing that well against a great team like Moeller, that I had a chance to play big-time college football.

We lost the McKinley game at the end of my sophomore year to finish 7–3 and fall short of the playoffs. But getting a taste of success made me even hungrier for the 1982 season and helped me formulate a new goal. I wanted to start at both linebacker and running back. I knew people doubted I could do it, but that just fueled my fire and made it more satisfying when I accomplished my goal. Our first game against Perry, I gained 130 yards on ten carries, played the entire game on defense, and returned punts.

We won that night and eleven more in a row, including a 7–0 win over McKinley to clinch a playoff berth at the end of my junior year. We won our first two playoff games to get to the state championship game, but we couldn't match up with Moeller. They dominated us, 35–12. I hated that feeling. I thought we had a shot because we had played them the year before, but once the game started, it became obvious they outclassed us. It would have taken a perfect game to beat them. They bottled me up pretty well on offense, so I started to get the idea that maybe I should concentrate on linebacker.

By now, plenty of colleges showed interest in recruiting me. I had followed Ohio State growing up, so I definitely planned to consider them. I also wanted to explore my options outside the Midwest. It felt pretty cool to get letters from USC, UCLA, Michigan, Penn State, and others. It floored me that those schools even knew about me.

That January, Wheaties cereal announced a national ad campaign called "Search for Champions." They planned to recognize six amateur athletes in the United States for their achievements and put each one on the cover of a box of Wheaties. I'm sure they also wanted to sell a lot of Wheaties, and the good people of Massillon eagerly obliged.

Massillon has about five booster clubs for its football team. One of them, CAATS—Concerned About All Tiger Sports—nominated me for the Wheaties contest. Once they did, boxes started to fly off the shelves all over town. People bought Wheaties just to get the ballots inside and send them in with my name. They ordered Wheaties by the truckload, a lot of which I'm sure they never ate, just because it helped get Massillon football some national recognition.

No one ever asked me if I wanted to be nominated. I really didn't. I just wanted everyone to leave me alone. But once the word got out, the thing took on a life of its own and became a tsunami, out of control. I had to make tons of appearances all over town. I signed Wheaties boxes at grocery stores, spoke at service clubs and luncheons … you name it, I did it. And every event made me want to withdraw more.

Right in the middle of that uncomfortable time, I met Stefanie Belcher. I will never forget that moment in the spring of 1983. I had just finished competing in the discus at a track meet when I looked up and saw her—the most beautiful female I had ever seen, right there in Canton, Ohio. I'm not exaggerating. In my eyes, she was the most stunning, striking, captivating, gorgeous female I had ever seen, not just in person, but ever.

I absolutely *had* to meet her.

Fortunately, a guy I knew also knew Stef, and he arranged for us to meet at a dance at a place called "The Barn." I had dated around a little bit, but nothing serious. I didn't really want to feel obligated with a relationship, and high school girls always required more of me in the way of phone calls or attention than I wanted to give.

Stef differed in at least a hundred ways from other girls. First, she just absolutely mesmerized me with her appearance. She had this way of fixing her hair differently every time I saw her, so it seemed like dating three girls at once. That made her unique, but she stood out from the crowd because she projected an air of genuine, complete confidence without the slightest trace of cockiness. She had a very secure self-image, far beyond someone just fifteen years old.

Although I was extremely shy, for whatever reason, I totally opened up to her. Looking back on the night we met, Stef always claimed she came over to me and said, "Are you looking for someone? I'm Stefanie." I recall that when we finally found each other, I cut in and stopped her from dancing with the quarterback from another high school. Our stories always differed. The only thing that really mattered was that we were together from that moment on.

I tried to get Stef to kiss me that night, but she hesitated. It sounds cheesy now and way more sinister than intended, but I tried to make a joke by reaching into my pocket and saying, "I'll give you a piece of candy if you let me kiss you." She laughed. So later that night, when I asked to drive her home and she begged off by telling me she came with friends, I said, "I'll give you a quarter if you let me drive you home."

The next night, I went over to her house and we sat on the swing, just talking. We seemed to feel the same way about everything, including the fact that she didn't want to go inside and I didn't want to go home. So we sat up all night, talking on the front porch. It shocked me that this amazing girl, beyond my dreams in every way, actually *liked* me.

Looking back, I know our relationship worked because Stef didn't smother me in any way. She had her friends and her interests, and she didn't need me fawning over her to feel secure. She was into modeling, dance, and cheerleading. I was into football, football, and football. We didn't see each other every day because she went to Jackson High School across town and I went to Massillon. I'd go over to her house about twice a week. She gave me someone to confide in and express my frustration.

I told her everything about how much I hated the attention I got from the Wheaties box contest, recruiting, and whatever else bothered me. We'd go on long walks together at Brookside Golf Course, near her house. With her, I could just be Chris, a seventeen-year-old kid.

My mom could sense my discomfort with the whole Wheaties situation, but no high school boy wants to confide in his mom. My silence around the house bothered her, and it bothered me because it bothered her. But at that age, I didn't feel comfortable telling my mom the same things I told Stef.

Any chance I had to be just a normal high school kid vanished once the Wheaties thing started. I had to visit sick kids in hospitals, sign autographs—all the stuff that drew me out against my will. Wherever I went, people stared at me. I felt like, *Is there something wrong with me? Why are these people looking at me?* I didn't realize they probably just thought, *Hey, that's the kid who might be on the Wheaties box*. I became very self-conscious and felt I couldn't live up to my own standard. Only Stef understood that, to me, the Wheaties campaign was far from a glorious, glamorous thing.

The time it bothered me the most came during a parade held in my honor. I hated that sort of stuff — another instance of calling attention to myself when I really wanted to vanish into the woodwork. I sat on this convertible as it cruised down the street, when I heard a woman say, "Hey, Spielman. Don't forget. This town *made* you." That infuriated me. I'd worked hard to achieve my success. It didn't come just because people bought boxes of Wheaties to get me an honor I didn't even want.

Despite feeling miserable off the field, on the field I had another good year as a senior. Our only loss came in the second game, 14 – 10, to Akron Garfield, but that ended up costing us a playoff berth. We finished with an 18 – 7 win over McKinley.

Thanks to the good people of Massillon, I easily made it into the top fifty vote-getters in the Wheaties competition. After that, a panel whittled it down to six winners based on athletic ability and personal character; somehow I ended up among the six. That earned me a trip to New York for the announcement at Tavern on the Green and, eventually, an appearance on the cover of a couple hundred thousand boxes distributed around the Midwest.

To this day, from time to time I still get Wheaties boxes in the mail to autograph.

Once my high school career ended, however, I had to stop stalling and pick where I would play college football.

I traveled to UCLA for my first recruiting trip. I'd never visited California, so that really opened my eyes. I saw a guy juggling chainsaws on Venice Beach. That sure didn't happen in Massillon! I went to UCLA's pre–Rose Bowl practices in my cowboy boots, trying to appear 6-foot–2, when I really stood just a shade over 6 feet. I stuffed those cowboy boots with wristbands, paper, whatever I could to give myself about three inches. One of their guys really stood out during the conditioning sprints. I asked, "Who's that linebacker?" They answered, "Oh, that's Donnie Rogers, our safety." That really humbled me, to realize a guy much bigger than I played safety in college.

I enjoyed my visit to UCLA, but I knew I wouldn't be happy there because of the distance from home. I also quickly eliminated Penn State, even though I loved Coach Joe Paterno. He came to my house and really charmed my mom. But I didn't like the campus, clear out there in the middle of nowhere.

Earle Bruce, the head coach at Ohio State, had served as head coach at my high school back in 1964 and 1965. His teams went 20–0, so the people of Massillon really revered Coach Bruce. He didn't hesitate to use his local popularity and contacts to put the heat on me. He told a luncheon at the Pro Football Hall of Fame in Canton, "Hey, if you see Spielman, tell him to go to Ohio State." I also found out Coach Bruce had friends in high places. One night, just as I got home, my mom met me at the door and said, "Chris, get in here. The governor is on the phone." Sure enough, it was Richard Celeste, the governor of the state of Ohio. I wish I'd had the political knowledge then that I do now. *That* would have been an interesting conversation. Instead, he did most of the talking, telling me why I should attend Ohio State.

Coach Bruce probably made it a priority to get me because he knew his chief rival, Bo Schembechler at Michigan, also wanted me. I loved Bo. He came from Stark County too, from Barberton. When I went up to Ann Arbor for my visit, Bo skipped out of a meeting with a player and his parents to meet with me. He told them, "I have to talk to this guy." Someone told me Bo never did that for anyone but me.

I really, *really* liked Michigan. They played Big Ten football, just like Ohio State, and I had enough rebel in me to warm to the idea of going against what everyone in Massillon wanted me to do—play for the Buckeyes in Columbus. The Wolverines played in the Sugar Bowl on January 1 that year. At halftime, one of the Michigan assistant coaches called me at home. That really made an impression on me. I thought, *Wow, they must really want me.*

I took my final visit to Miami, which had just won the national championship for the 1983 season. Bernie Kosar, their quarterback and a Youngstown guy, hosted me that weekend. But Miami had no shot at getting me after I found out its head coach, Howard Schnel-lenberger, didn't even bother to stay in town for my visit. That trip served only one purpose: It gave me some time away so I could decide between Ohio State and Michigan.

While I debated my choice on the flight home, I had to change planes in Dayton. Back then, you didn't need a ticket to go through security and walk the concourses. I left my plane and started walking to my connection when I came upon this crowd of Ohio State fans. They had signs plastered with my name on them and chanted, "We want Chris! We want Chris!" I didn't need that. The Wheaties campaign had made me self-conscious enough. No high school kid wants to call attention to himself, and I had a greater desire to fly under the radar than most kids my age. I appreciated that these people wanted me to play for their team, but they went about it in the wrong way. While it showed me the fanaticism of Ohio State's supporters, mostly it just embarrassed me. They followed me every step of the way down the corridor. I couldn't wait to board my flight and get out of there.

Finally, the night before national signing day, we had a basketball game against Akron Hoban (I started for three years in basketball). Three of the schools on my list of finalists sent assistant coaches to watch from the stands: Milan Vooletich from Michigan, Booker Brooks of Penn State, and the offensive coordinator at Ohio State, Glen Mason. By then, UCLA and Miami had given up. But the other three schools wouldn't allow me to get away without sending a guy to ask one last time, "What's your decision?"

After the game, I told each one that I had to go home and think about it some more. When I got home, I went back and forth in my mind between Ohio State and Michigan. About 12:30 in the morning, my dad came into my room and said, "What's it going to be?"

"I don't know, Dad," I replied. "I really like Michigan. I think I want to go there."

He looked hard at me and responded, "I'll tell you where you're going. You're going straight down I–71 south to Ohio State. That's where you're going. Get on the phone and call those other coaches, and then call Coach Bruce."

My dad had waited for me to make the right decision, so long as that decision agreed with his. He grew up in Ohio and coached at the Ohio State coaching clinic for years. He couldn't possibly allow his son to reject the Ohio State Buckeyes for the Michigan Wolverines.

It actually came as a relief once my dad jumped me like that. Ohio State made the most sense. Once he put it that way, I could see it so clearly. Michigan played to my personality: "Be different. Be a rebel. Set your own path. Don't do what everyone else does." They used an effective recruiting strategy, and I almost fell for it.

I called the assistant coaches from Michigan and Penn State to let them know my decision. I couldn't very well wake up Bo Schembechler or Joe Paterno at that hour to tell them I'd chosen Ohio State. Once I got that out of the way, I dialed Coach Bruce to let him know that his full-court press on everyone from Massillon had worked. I could tell from the way he answered the phone that he'd been asleep when I called. "Coach," I said, "this is Chris Spielman. I've made my decision."

Then I paused, messing with him a little.

"I've decided to come to Ohio State."

Coach Bruce didn't see the humor in my little joke. I could tell from the tone of his voice when he said, "Oh, you wait 'til I get my hands on you down here, boy. I'll get you for that."

I thought, OK, *no more kidding around with Coach Bruce.*

My dad made me do a press conference the next day at the Massillon City School District administration building. I didn't want to do it; I wanted to remain invisible. I even had to wear this ridiculous sweat suit with my high school number, 33, on it. I had grown so tired of the attention and all the hoopla about where I would go to college. I wanted nothing more than for everyone to leave me alone.

I didn't realize then that as the No. 1 recruit of the Ohio State Buckeyes, my days with privacy had ended.

CHAPTER 7

TOUGH TIMES ON CAMPUS

SOMETIMES, REALIZING A LIFELONG DREAM FALLS SHORT OF EXPEC-
tations. I learned that the hard way just prior to reporting to Ohio
State for my freshman season in 1984.

I'd always wanted to play in the Ohio North-South All-Star game
because, as a kid, I went there every year on my summer vacation. My
dad served as the equipment manager for the game, so he would take
Rick and me and we'd spend the week in the Walsh College dorms
with the guys about to play in the game. I idolized those guys as much
as I did anyone in college or the NFL. When Todd Blackledge played
for the North in 1978, I caught passes from him in practice. I figured
if, as a twelve-year-old, I could catch fastballs from a guy who signed
to play quarterback at Penn State, then I'd never drop another ball.

It felt so cool to be up close and personal with those guys. They
lived in the dorms, ate in the cafeteria, went through two-a-day practices—and so did I. It made me feel like I belonged there and fed my
fantasies about becoming a professional football player.

Now I had made it to that very same all-star game, and so had my
future Ohio State teammates William White, Tom Tupa, Jeff Uhlenhake, and Scott Powell. My fantasy had come true—right up to the
moment someone rolled on my ankle and sprained it in the first half
of the game. So with the dream of playing in the North-South game
came the nightmare of getting hurt just three weeks before the start
of my first training camp at Ohio State.

I knew about the oversized expectations OSU's fans had for me,
but no one had bigger expectations than I had for myself. If I wanted

71

to reach my goal of playing in the NFL, I had to take the next step and excel on the college level. I didn't intend to fail, but it didn't help that my ankle still felt pretty tender. Freshmen reported early back then, so we had a few days to get acclimated to how things worked before the varsity showed up. Once that happened, all the internal pressure I put on myself got a boost from the crap I started taking from the upperclassmen.

At our first meeting of the whole squad, freshmen had to stand up and introduce themselves.

"Chris Spielman, Massillon, Ohio," I said.

Then the catcalls started.

They made cracks about the Wheaties box, about my voice, about anything and everything.

That only fueled my fire. The chip on my shoulder that I brought to Columbus grew into a tree trunk. No one else put it there. I put it there. I knew all the accolades I received in high school would force me to make a mark early or get eaten up. I had to prove myself, and I couldn't wait to get after it.

Having started every game I'd ever played before coming to Ohio State, it bummed me out when, on the first day of practice, they assigned me to the third team. I understood, because they had returning players who already had proven themselves. But I didn't like it. All the offensive linemen said to me, "We'll show you when the pads go on, rookie." I just said, "Hey, I'm not going anywhere. I'll be right here."

When we finally went full-go for the first time, I treated it like my own personal Super Bowl. Playing on the scout team essentially made me human cannon fodder for the starters and backups. That didn't deter me one bit. I flew around and made plays, hoping to demonstrate to the coaches what I could do. It must have worked, because they promoted me to second team that afternoon, which enabled me to start practicing with the varsity.

The returning linebackers were Pepper Johnson, Larry Kolic, Fred Ridder, Mark Pfister, and Bill Harvey. We played a 3–4 alignment on defense. Pepper and Larry started inside, where I wanted to play. To get on the field, I would have to beat someone out. By the time we held our first scrimmage in Ohio Stadium, I had two weeks of practice under my belt against our offense. That, combined with being a coach's son and watching game films as long as I could remember, helped me know the plays before the snap. I jumped on everything. I knew where our quarterback, Mike Tomczak, intended to go with the ball. I knew where he would throw against every coverage. I knew Coach Bruce and the plays he liked to run. I anticipated the fullback blast up the middle and when they would pitch it wide to our tailback, Keith Byars. I knew Coach and Mike loved the Y Shallow route to the tight end, Ed Taggart, across the middle. I knew if I dropped back and gave Mike a look like I would bite on the Dig, but then jumped the tight end, I would make the play. From my perspective, that scrimmage went about as well as it could have gone.

They gave us Saturday night off, so I drove home to Massillon to see Stef. When I returned to Columbus the next day, Coach Bruce pulled me aside and said, "You're starting the opener against Oregon State in two weeks." I'd proven my point. I'd positioned myself to start my college career just the way I'd hoped. So far, everything had gone according to plan.

But then, one week before the opener, at the end of our last scrimmage, someone rolled onto the same ankle I'd hurt in the North-South game. I sprained it again.

I was livid. I kept asking, "Why? Why me? Why now?" I had no perspective at all, because in my mind, the biggest game of my life was just a week away. I'd not only lost the starting spot I'd worked so hard to earn, but now I couldn't even practice. The disappointment threw me into a funk. I started acting like a spoiled brat. While my teammates got ready to play Oregon State, I sulked around, feeling sorry for myself. I'd like to say my attitude improved as we got closer to kickoff, but it didn't. I pouted all night before the game, the morning of the game, and up to and including the first half of the game.

I can't believe I did this now, but throughout the first and second quarters, I paced right behind Coach Bruce on the sideline, venting about not getting to play. I stomped around, making sure he would hear me say, "You've gotta put me in. This is why you recruited me. I've got to be out there." He probably would have ignored me if our defense had played better, but we fell behind and trailed late in the first half. He let me go in either to fix the problem or maybe just to shut me up. I didn't know why and I didn't care why. Finally I was out there.

The first play, we called a blitz with me stunting. Oregon State failed to pick it up, and I sacked the quarterback. Coach Bruce put me back out there in the second half, and we came from behind to win. I didn't accomplish my goal of starting my first game, but I finished with ten tackles and won back my job.

We played Washington State the next week, and I played OK. We won to go 2–0. Then Iowa came to town for our Big Ten opener. In the first quarter, *bam*, I hurt the same ankle. Someone rolled on it again, only this time it hurt more than before.

I handled it as maturely as you might expect. I whined and complained like I did when they canceled the final game of my eighth-grade football season. That night in my dorm room in Park Hall, I smashed my crutches against the wall. I completely lost it. The disappointment consumed me. I wanted to play! That's all I cared about. I felt like if I couldn't play, I had no value to the team, myself, or anyone else.

I was really immature.

I went into seclusion and stopped eating. I'd look at calendars on campus and see "September 22." "That's the day I got hurt," I'd say to myself. Classes hadn't started yet, so I sat around and thought about the injustice of getting hurt after working so hard to win a job. Thinking only of myself, I went into Coach Bruce's office one day and asked him if I should redshirt—sit out the rest of the season and preserve my first year of eligibility for the next year.

He went nuts.

"That's selfish," he railed at me. "You don't get to make that decision!"

About that time, my dad came down to visit. He grabbed me by the throat and told me, in so many words, to stop feeling sorry for myself and straighten up. By then, my weight had dropped to around 200 pounds, about twenty less than when I'd reported.

When you're eighteen years old, everything seems magnified far beyond its actual importance. I'd dreamed of playing college football and getting to the NFL my whole life. Obviously, a sprained ankle couldn't keep me from doing that. But I magnified it to the point where it felt like the world was crashing in around me.

It took four weeks before I could get healthy enough to play again, this time against Michigan State. Of course, I hurt the ankle again. I thought, *I'm cursed* or just a big sissy. A team doctor suggested I try orthotics in my shoes. That seemed to help, or maybe the three weeks I sat out made the difference. The ankle at least healed enough that I could practice a bit for our last regular-season game against Michigan.

I wanted to be a force against our archrival and the school I almost picked over Ohio State. Instead, I played only a little in the second half of a victory that gave us the Big Ten championship and a berth in the Rose Bowl against USC.

Coach Bruce told Larry, Pepper, and me that we would have an open competition for the inside linebacker jobs when bowl practice started in three weeks. By then, my ankle had improved and I could play without any limits. I won back my job and got to fly first-class with the rest of the starters to the West Coast.

We went into the game ranked No. 6 to USC's No. 18, but they jumped on us early and had a 17–6 lead at halftime. Our four turnovers killed us in a 20–17 loss. I recovered a fumble and had fifteen tackles, but ending the season that way brought a frustrating end to a frustrating year. All my injuries removed a lot of the joy from my first season because I didn't feel I had contributed much to our success.

I didn't know then that this would be my only outright Big Ten championship and my only trip to the Rose Bowl. If I had known it, I would have enjoyed it more.

That summer of 1985, I went over to Stef's house one day, planning to go with her and her family to visit her younger sister, Sandy, at camp. Just as we got ready to leave, her father, Dr. Richard Belcher, collapsed in their living room. Out of nowhere, he started having a seizure. That led to the discovery of a brain tumor, which severely limited him physically once he returned to his dermatology practice. It broke Stef's heart to watch him struggle and try to recover.

She planned to try out for cheerleader at Ohio State that fall, but decided against it because of her dad's cancer. Stef realized how little time he might have left, so she visited home a lot to spend as much time with him as possible.

I loved having her on campus with me. Stef gave me the freedom to be a psycho football freak, and I gave her the freedom to do the things she wanted. I trusted her so much I never gave it a second thought when she went to sorority dances with other guys. If I didn't want to go or had a football commitment, I'd suggest she find somebody else. None of that ever offended her. She never said, "What's the matter with you?" At least, she never said it until we got married. Then she said it a few times.

The close loss to USC in the Rose Bowl, combined with the players we had returning for my sophomore year, had us really excited about what we could accomplish in 1985. We had Keith Byars, the Heisman Trophy runner-up, at tailback, and Cris Carter, who set a Rose Bowl receiving yardage record, at wide receiver. Pepper, Larry, and I returned at linebacker, so we looked pretty solid on defense. But all that optimism took a big hit in preseason camp when Keith broke a bone in his foot in a noncontact drill. That became the most famous fifth metatarsal—the bone on the outside of his foot—in history.

We started 5–1, but teams put up such incredible passing numbers against us that Burt Graeff of the Columbus *Citizen-Journal* wrote that we might give up 1,000 yards passing when No. 1 Iowa and their quarterback, Chuck Long, came to town. Instead, we put a serious dent in Chuck's Heisman campaign by intercepting him four times and upsetting Iowa in a driving rainstorm. I had two of the picks and made a big fourth-down stop deep in our territory. The stadium had unbelievable energy that day. The atmosphere fired me up so much that on one play, I couldn't get my chinstrap to fasten, so I just ripped off my helmet and made the tackle without any headgear.

That win moved us up to No. 4 in the polls. We stood at No. 3

two weeks later when Wisconsin came to town and upset us, 12–7. That was the second straight year (and the fourth time in five years) Wisconsin beat us. Those guys really had our number.

The loss left us needing a win at Michigan the following week— along with an Iowa loss to Minnesota—to return to the Rose Bowl. We didn't get either one. John Kolesar beat us on a long touchdown pass from Jim Harbaugh, so we headed off to the Citrus Bowl in Orlando to play Brigham Young on January 1.

BYU had a great quarterback in Robbie Bosco, who had led them to the national championship two years before. He came into the Citrus Bowl having thrown for more than 4,000 yards and thirty touchdowns that season, so everyone figured he would torch our secondary.

Coach Bruce had a little surprise for Robbie. We'd worked on a new defense in the spring called the Tennessee Bubble. It used three inside linebackers, with Pepper and me playing our normal spots and Larry playing a stand-up nose guard. We didn't use it much during the regular season, but maybe we should have, judging by how well it worked against BYU. We had a great read on Bosco. Every time he turned his shoulders dropping back, he threw to his right. Every time he did a straight drop-back, he threw to his left. That key held true through the whole game, and we shut down their offense. Larry intercepted two passes and returned one for our only touchdown. We picked Bosco off two more times in the end zone and won, 10–7.

That win extended our streak of 9–3 records to six years, so we wanted to avoid another one of those in 1986. After two games, though, we gladly would have settled for another 9–3 season.

Alabama beat us, 16–10, in the Kickoff Classic in New Jersey in the opener. Then we went to Washington and got killed, 40–7. So, after starting out ranked in the Top Ten, we dropped out of the rankings and had to win six straight just to get back in.

One of those victories came against Illinois, 14–0, in our Big Ten opener. The week of the game, Coach Bruce asked me to visit a fifteen-year-old kid from Upper Arlington, Will McClure, who had suffered a spine injury in a football game. I had a nice conversation with Will. We talked about the Illinois game and I said, "Hey, maybe I'll get a pick." Sure enough, late in the game, they ran a Dig and I had a good, deep drop that put me in position to make the interception. I kept the game ball and took it to Will in the hospital.

By the time Michigan came to Columbus for the final game of the regular season, we had won nine in a row and had worked our way back to No. 7 in the country. The last of those wins came against Wisconsin, which had owned us. I punched my fist through a chalkboard in the locker room just before kickoff that day in Madison; I wanted to beat those guys so bad, and we did. That same day in Ann Arbor, Minnesota upset Michigan, which really didn't change anything, other than to knock Michigan down in the rankings. We hadn't lost a game in the Big Ten, and they had only one loss, so the winner of our game would go to the Rose Bowl. If we won, we'd be the outright conference champions. I *really* wanted that. And I wanted to avenge our loss to Michigan the year before. I wanted it even more on Monday after Michigan's quarterback, Jim Harbaugh, guaranteed his team would beat us that Saturday.

We trailed by only two points midway through the fourth quarter when I forced a fumble. Our offense moved the ball to Michigan's 28-yard line, and on fourth down Coach Bruce sent our kicker, Matt Frantz, in for a field goal attempt to win the game, win the conference, and send us to the Rose Bowl. I celebrated on the sidelines as we lined up—but then I saw the kick. Matt hooked it left. I don't remember exactly what I said to him, probably something like, "You're a kicker! You've got one job. MAKE THE KICK!" But Matt didn't lose the game for us. He could have turned around and said something like, "You have one job. Keep them from rushing for 500 yards and we might have a chance." And he'd have been absolutely right.

I had twenty-nine tackles that day and tied an Ohio State single-game record. But I made that many tackles only because Jamie Morris ran all over us. We shouldn't have been on the field that long. And the twenty-nine tackles didn't mean anything. We lost the game. We lost the championship. And we went 9–3 again.

Technically, we tied Michigan for the Big Ten championship, but they went to Pasadena and we headed to the Cotton Bowl to play Texas A&M.

In those days, the Cotton Bowl ranked as one of the four major bowl games. Texas A&M came in ranked No. 8 to our No. 11 ranking, giving us a chance for an upset to mask some of our frustration over losing to Michigan. A&M had a great team, full of future NFL players; but I grew tired of hearing about the Aggies from the Texas sportswriters who showed up to cover the game. One day I lost it. "What are we, a bunch of bozos? Are we crap? We'll find out. We'll line up and play and find out who's tougher."

Coach Bruce surprised everyone that New Year's Day by wearing a suit and a fedora on the sidelines. We tried to match him fashion-wise by wearing red shoes, but it wouldn't have mattered if we wore polka-dot shoes. We had Texas A&M completely confused. We played five linebackers, two defensive linemen, and four defensive backs. Their quarterback, Kevin Murray, couldn't figure out what we were in and stared down his receivers all day. I had two of our five interceptions, including one early in the third quarter that I took back for a touchdown and a 14–6 lead. I hadn't returned an interception for a touchdown since I was nine years old in midget league football back in Canton.

We ended up winning, 28–12, which gave us ten wins. That really thrilled Coach Bruce. "There won't be any more of this 9–3 crap," he said afterward. "This is a new year, a new start for the Ohio State Buckeyes."

Little did he, or we, know that January 1 would turn out to be nearly the only day of that year when things would go right for the Buckeyes.

CHAPTER 8

A SEASON OF LOSS

No one could have predicted how many things would go wrong my senior year. I doubt any previous Ohio State team ever suffered as much adversity as we did that season, and it started almost as soon as we got back from the Cotton Bowl in Dallas.

Coach Bruce didn't travel home with us; he went directly to the national coaches' convention. The University of Arizona approached him there about taking over as its head coach. We all knew Coach Bruce didn't want to leave Ohio State, but Arizona came after him hard, and OSU made no effort to sweeten his contract or prove to him it wanted him to stay. Coach had two years left on his deal, and Ohio State didn't offer to extend it. That sent a clear message the administration had entered a wait-and-see mode in regard to Coach Bruce's future at Ohio State.

Coach Bruce was just combative enough not to care. After all, we had high hopes for 1987. We had Cris coming off an All-American season at wide receiver and me returning at linebacker. If Coach had known what would happen in July, he might have taken the Arizona job in January. But he didn't know, so he didn't go.

That spring, I got a call from some guy asking me if I had any interest in meeting with some agents on campus looking at potential NFL players. By now, I had a pretty good idea I would realize my dream of playing professional football, so I thought, *Why not?* I met with the guy, who showed me an envelope full of cash. "This is yours if you commit to our agency," he said. I didn't have much money, but the offer didn't tempt me. I thought, *Why would I do that now?* It didn't seem right and it just didn't make sense. I told no one about the offer. I just turned around and walked away.

Not everyone rejected that temptation. Agents from New York, Chicago, and Los Angeles tried to get a jump on the market that year by signing college players to postdated representation agreements. The players agreed to the deals that spring and summer, but the contracts made it appear the players had waited to sign until after their college careers. The agents used cash, airline tickets, and other inducements to get the players' signatures.

The scandal broke wide open that summer, when we found out Cris had signed with an agent and accepted money in violation of NCAA rules. Some players at other schools paid back the money and had their eligibility restored so they could play their senior year. Cris didn't get that opportunity; I still don't know why.

Now, a month before training camp, we had this huge hole in our lineup. As the best receiver in college football, Cris already held the Ohio State career receiving record after playing just three years. Everyone on our team, and all of our opponents, knew what Cris meant to us. One incident from my junior year perfectly demonstrated that.

Our coaches wouldn't allow anyone to hit Cris in practice because of his importance to our success. He knew that, and sometimes he took advantage of it. One day, I saw him ducking his shoulder and running over our defensive backs after he caught a pass. Cris liked to joke around. He liked to toy with his buddies in the secondary. That would have been fine if they could have hit him back, but they couldn't.

The coaches started yelling at us like they did in every drill, encouraging us to get physical with the receivers. I knew that didn't apply to hitting Cris, but I decided to do it anyway. He came across the middle on a slant route, so I gave him a good shot to even things out a little. I didn't take him to the ground, but I whacked him good just to stick up for my guys on defense and send a little message: "Hey, don't be hitting them if they can't hit you." Coach Bruce didn't take kindly to my vigilante justice. He drove up in his golf cart, called my name, and ordered me off to the side.

"Don't you know how important he is to our football team?" he asked, his voice rising. "Don't you lay a hand on him." I already knew that, but just to make sure I knew it, Coach had me do a set of Buckeye Reminders. I ran five yards, hit the deck, got up, ran five more, hit the deck again … all the way down the field. Coach Bruce drove his cart right beside me the whole time, lecturing me about being selfish. I did those Buckeye Reminders long enough that the message became clear: "Cris is a crucial part of our team, and if he wants to run over our defensive backs in practice, let him do it."

But now that he'd lost his eligibility in the agent scandal, Cris couldn't run over any defensive backs—ours or our opponents'. When I heard the news, I got mad at him. He'd always been a tough competitor and a conscientious guy, but he made a bad mistake and now our team would suffer for it. If Cris could have taken it back, he would have, but he couldn't. We would have to pay a big price for his mistake, because in losing him we lost our best player. You're conditioned to look at something like that just as you would an injury: "We don't have him. There's nothing we can do, so we go forward. The train keeps chugging down the track." That sounds great—but really, everything we did on offense revolved around him. We didn't have anyone even close to his caliber as a replacement. Guys tried, but you can't replace Cris Carter.

He and I never talked about his choice and what it cost our team until twenty-three years later. By then, we both worked for ESPN as football analysts and were in Bristol together when another agent situation came up in college football. Eric Kuselias, who hosted *Mike & Mike in the Morning*, asked Cris and me to sit in and talk about our experience with agents in college. It made me feel better to hear Cris talk about how much he regretted what happened our senior year and how, if given the choice, he would rather have played that final season at Ohio State than win a Super Bowl in the NFL. I wasn't surprised he said that, because I knew how much being an Ohio State Buckeye meant to him.

The next blow was a personal one. Right before training camp my senior year, Stef's father lost his battle with brain cancer. I admired

Dr. Belcher immensely, but for different reasons than I admired my father. Stef's dad enjoyed classical music and the arts. He was very gentle and caring as the only man in a house of five women. They all adored him, and he adored them. I had such enormous respect for him that I always called him Dr. Belcher; nothing else seemed right. His death really hurt Stef, and it hurt me too. She and I had been dating for four years, and I had grown very close to her dad.

Dr. Belcher fought for two years before the cancer finally won. Stef and I were at the hospital when they told us we should go in to say our good-byes. I promised him I would always love and care for his daughter and would protect her forever. It's still very hard for me to fight the feeling, however irrational, that I failed to keep that promise because I couldn't keep cancer from taking Stef away from me and our children.

The only time I ever saw Stef break down in all the years I knew her was the day her father died. Nothing she experienced over the course of her own twelve-year battle with breast cancer ever impacted her outwardly like losing her dad. But that traumatic event also crystallized her faith and fortified the foundation she needed to handle the challenges she would face. During those Ohio State years, we both searched for answers. We knew what we believed spiritually, but I doubt either of us understood why we believed it. We wanted answers.

Growing up in God-fearing homes had taught us that the basis of our faith rested on Jesus' death on the cross and in His resurrection. We needed to understand *why* His death paid the debt for our sin, a debt we couldn't pay ourselves. We needed to understand *why* His resurrection proved His power over death and provided eternal life for all who would believe in Him.

We started gaining an understanding of the plan of salvation by attending meetings of Fellowship of Christian Athletes at Ohio State. Still, we didn't have that one "aha" moment when everything clicked. Our spiritual growth progressed more deliberately, with both of us feeding off each other as we talked about what we were learning. As that took place, it definitely deepened our love as a couple.

After all the bad things that had happened both on and off the field, I hoped the start of the 1987 season would bring things back to normal. I wanted to end my Ohio State career on a high note. We started the season ranked No. 5 in the nation and defeated West Virginia and Oregon at home. That set up a Top Ten matchup at LSU the following week. Ohio State had never played LSU, so the game had a tremendous buildup. We heard all about how tough it would be to play in Death Valley, and everything we heard came true. That place was deafening! Their crowd tried to intimidate us, but Coach Bruce wouldn't have it. He refused to leave the locker room until LSU had taken the field. He didn't want us out there when LSU ran on and their crowd went nuts. The TV people ordered us out, but Coach Bruce wouldn't budge.

When we finally took the field for the coin toss, I immediately took a strong dislike to one of LSU's offensive linemen, Eric Andolsek. The way he acted, trying to look all mean and nasty, just ticked me off. I said, "Who are you trying to intimidate?" It just went to blows from there. We pushed and shoved and threw haymakers at each other. It was testosterone at its highest level. The game ended in a 13–13 tie when LSU blocked a field goal attempt on the final play. The tie disappointed us, but tying the No. 4 team in the country at their place didn't indicate we had any major problems.

We should have noticed that our offense struggled to score in every one of our first four games. Illinois held us to ten points in the league opener, but we squeaked by with a four-point win. After that, the losses started piling up, beginning with a 31–10 rout by Indiana in Ohio Stadium. Woody Hayes lost to Indiana in the Horseshoe his first season in 1951 and vowed he would never lose to them again. He didn't, nor did Coach Bruce through his first eight years. That explains why Coach Bruce called the loss "the darkest day in Ohio State history."

It didn't take long for things to get even darker. We beat Purdue and Minnesota to set up a first-place showdown at home against Michigan State. Our offense scored on an eighty-yard pass on the first play from scrimmage, but MSU came back to beat us, 13–7, to take control of the conference race.

Maybe we felt hung over from that loss, but what happened the following week at Wisconsin sent us spiraling down the drain. Our offense turned it over seven times, six in the second half, to blow a 24–13 halftime lead. Wisconsin took one interception back for a touchdown, and two other turnovers (at our nineteen and twenty-nine yard lines) set up field goals. We fumbled two kickoffs that day. And despite all that, we had a twenty-two-yard field goal attempt to win ... and we missed it. That's how you lose to a 3–6 team that comes into the game as an eighteen-point underdog. In the locker room afterward, I told reporters, "This is the lowest point of my career."

Iowa came to Ohio Stadium the following Saturday for Senior Day, my final game in the Horseshoe. The heat had built up on Coach Bruce because of our 5–3–1 record and the ineptitude of our offense over the previous two weeks. He badly needed a win to get the critics off his back, and I didn't want to go out a loser in my last home game. The lead changed hands five times that day and we led, 27–22, with Iowa on offense and time for one last play, from our twenty-eight yard line.

I called the defense in the huddle—man-to-man coverage—and told my teammates, "This is it. This is the last play of the last game I'll ever play in this stadium." No Ohio State fan will ever forget that play ... but not for pleasant reasons. Chuck Hartlieb threw to his tight end, Marv Cook, at the ten yard line. Cook evaded our defensive back, cut inside one of our safeties, and dragged the other safety into the end zone as time ran out. Final score: Iowa 29, Ohio State 27. We lost for the third straight week to fall to 3–4 in the Big Ten, OSU's worst conference record in twenty-one years.

All the hoopla started after that. Fans blamed Coach Bruce and debated his status all weekend. He took his wife, Jean, to his press conference on Monday, something he'd never done before. He pounded his fist on the table when he talked about how honorable the men on Ohio State's Board of Trustees were. For that reason, he said, he expected them to honor the final season of his contract the following year.

He didn't know that at that very moment, OSU President Edward Jennings was informing Rick Bay, our athletic director, that Coach Bruce would be fired after our final game at Michigan. President Jennings wanted Rick to stay quiet about it until the next week, but Rick went public with the news and resigned in protest.

I heard the news in my apartment just as I got ready to leave for practice. Coach Bruce called a team meeting later that day and said, "This is not going to take away from your preparation for the Michigan game." To watch him that week, you'd never have known he'd just lost his job. He went about preparing us to win just as hard as he always did—and never once did he mention anything along the lines of "Oh, woe is me." I found that honorable. I also found it very useful later when life threw me difficult challenges.

Oddly enough, the way Coach Bruce's firing happened turned him from everyone's favorite whipping boy into a hero. It outraged Ohio State fans that the school fired him five days before the Michigan game. One local television station ran a poll asking viewers who had their support, Coach Bruce or President Jennings. Coach got 90 percent of the votes. The criticism from the public grew so strong that Dr. Jennings, I suppose in an attempt to get some good publicity, called me and our other captain, William White, in to explain the firing to us. We knew it amounted to a token meeting, since we had no power to change anything, no matter how much support we voiced for Coach Bruce.

Everyone knows the rules when they enter the world of big-time college football. I knew how the game worked. Coaches get fired, whether fair or not. I came from Massillon, where coaches got fired all the time. Why waste my breath in some trumped-up meeting with the school president? I just sat there and didn't say much.

All the furor of Coach Bruce's firing made the week of practice fly by. Before I knew it, Friday had arrived and, with it, Senior Tackle, an Ohio State tradition. All the seniors get one last crack at the blocking sled the day before the Michigan game. The local television stations come in to film it for the news that night. Someone told me that an injury had prevented Coach Bruce from participating in Senior Tackle when he played at Ohio State. So, once all our seniors had taken their turn, I grabbed the microphone. "Coach, you never got the chance to do this, so now's your shot." Man, did he fire out of his stance and hit that thing. I saw the smile on his face and knew we couldn't have done anything better for him.

The best thing, of course, would have been to win the Michigan game and send Coach Bruce out a winner. Neither Michigan nor Ohio State was ranked in the Top 20, the first time that had happened in twenty-one years. Still, no one who's ever played in that game needs rankings or bowl bids or anything else to make it the most important college game they've ever played. Two years earlier, after the '85 Chicago Bears won the Super Bowl, their quarterback Jim McMahon popularized wearing headbands with messages printed on them. One of our offensive linemen, Joe Staysniak, masterminded a plan to get everyone on the team a headband with "EARLE" printed in bold, black letters. We snuck them onto our heads after we came in from pregame warm-up and ran out onto the field for the coin toss. We sprinted to the south end zone, and then everyone took off their helmets to reveal the headbands. Any other day, any other game, Coach Bruce never would have put up with that. But that day, I think he got a charge out of it.

We started out like we should have worn headbands with "HELP" written on them instead. Michigan scored on its first three possessions to lead 13–0. Our offense couldn't move the ball, but finally drove for a touchdown just before halftime. Despite being outgained in the first half, 281–91, we trailed only 13–7.

That changed on the first play of the second half, when Carlos Snow took a screen pass for a touchdown. A little later our offense scored again, but we missed the extra point and led by just a touchdown, 20–13. Michigan tied it, and we got the ball at the fourteen yard line with twelve minutes left. Our offense came up big, chewing seven minutes off the clock before we sent Matt Frantz on for a twenty-six-yard field goal attempt.

The year before, Matt had missed a forty-five yarder in the last minute of the loss that cost us an outright Big Ten championship and a trip to the Rose Bowl. Because of that, he told the *Ann Arbor News* the week of the game, "For 11 months, I've been known as 'Matt, the guy who lost the Michigan game.' Of course I'd like another chance at them. I know it sounds selfish, but I'd like it to come down to that last kick again." He got his wish, and he didn't blow it. He made the kick to give us a 23–20 lead with five minutes left.

Michigan moved to midfield, but then LeRoy Hoard fumbled and Eric Kumerow recovered. We ran out all but the final seconds for an emotional win in Coach Bruce's final game. I thought about helping the guys carry him off the field, but instead I stood off to the side and watched. Just looking at him, seeing the smile on his face and the pride he had in that win, helped make up for some of the disappointment over our 6–4–1 record my senior year.

CHAPTER 9

THE DREAM BEGINS

I LOVED THE FEELING OF BEATING MICHIGAN TO END MY COLLEGE career, even though the season fell far short of my expectations. The Sun Bowl extended an invitation for us to play in El Paso, but the Ohio State administration wouldn't allow Coach Bruce or an interim replacement to coach that game. Still, with the way things unfolded the week of the Michigan game—with Coach Bruce getting fired and all the drama that accompanied it—we ended on as high a note as possible. No one would have remembered or cared much about how we fared in the Sun Bowl. Our 6–4–1 record didn't measure up to the typical Ohio State standard, but I'm still proud of that team and my role as captain, no matter what people said or thought about us.

The losses always seemed to overshadow the wins in my football career. We lost in the state championship game at Massillon, and we didn't win a national championship at Ohio State. I had a hard time letting that go because I took it personally. I always thought, *If I would have done this . . . if I would have done that . . .*

But I had to put aside the disappointment of the 1987 season and focus on getting ready for the NFL draft and the job I'd dreamed about as long as I could remember—being a professional football player.

Every draft hopeful looks for whatever edge he can get. I hoped it would increase my appeal to the NFL when I won the Lombardi Trophy, given to the nation's most outstanding lineman or linebacker. I flew to Houston with my parents for the banquet. As an old-school guy, I loved winning a trophy with Vince Lombardi's name on it. Awards like that are never individual things; they're team things, particularly at linebacker. I led the nation in tackles only because my linemen did a great job of occupying blockers to keep me free from contact. I thanked them for that in my acceptance speech. Coach Bruce sat on the dais with me and said some very nice things about me: "He has the most intensity of any player I've ever been around. He's a guy who never stepped out of line."

I guess Coach forgot about me giving Cris Carter that shot in practice.

Once I returned from the Lombardi banquet, I set my sights on playing in the Japan Bowl against other draft-eligible seniors. My dad had a conversation with John McVey, the general manager of the San Francisco 49ers and a guy he coached with at Canton Central Catholic. McVey told my dad I really needed to play in the Senior Bowl. But since I thought it would be cool to go to Japan, I committed to going over there instead. I knew I needed to get on tape against top-level competition so the scouts could compare me to other guys. I figured I could do that in Tokyo as well as in Mobile, Alabama. Why not take the free trip to Japan?

I figured NFL scouts would pour over that Japan Bowl film, so I really wanted to do well. My plans took a hit when doctors told me my right ring finger needed surgery to repair a torn tendon suffered during the season. Knowing how the NFL obsessed over injuries, I thought I should get the finger repaired right away, and I pulled out of the trip to Japan for that reason. But once I talked to the doctors about the specifics of surgery, I discovered the recovery time would mess up my training for the NFL Scouting Combine. By the time I decided to delay the surgery, I couldn't get back into the Japan Bowl. And because I initially committed to playing in Japan, I couldn't get into the Senior Bowl either. The whole thing added up to one gigantic mistake. Had I played well in either place, it really would have boosted my draft stock. Not playing in either all-star game put all the pressure on my performance at the Combine in Indianapolis.

I'd dropped out of school after fall quarter so I could devote all my time to getting ready for the NFL. I tried hard to attack my training, but I couldn't help myself much from a nutritional perspective. I didn't have a job, so I had no money in my food budget. Fortunately, Jim Lachey, an All-American offensive lineman on our Rose Bowl team from 1984, came back to town and stopped at my apartment one day. I asked Jim if he wanted a peanut butter sandwich. "Sure," he said. After all, what NFL offensive lineman is going to turn down a sandwich? I had some bread I bought for nineteen cents off the bargain rack. When I started spreading the peanut butter on it, the stale bread fell to pieces. I handed this lump of peanut butter to Jim, with crumbs and flakes of bread stuck to it. He took one look and said, "Let's go."

I thought he wanted to go to a restaurant to get something to eat, but instead Jim drove me to Bank One in downtown Columbus. In my entire life, I'd never visited a bank. I had a job in high school, but I just gave the check to my mom or dad and they cashed it for me. In college, I paid cash for everything. I had no experience with any of this banking stuff.

Jim went up to a bank employee, pointed to me, and said, "He wants to open a checking account." I didn't have any money for that, but Jim wrote a check for $2,000 and deposited it in my account. He certainly didn't have to do that for me. But that gave me the money I needed to eat better in preparation for the Combine and sure took a lot of pressure off my preparations for Indianapolis.

The Combine is part cattle call and part inquisition. First comes the detailed medical exam. When that ends, you strip down to your shorts and stand in a room full of scouts, who listen to a guy reading off all your vital statistics. NFL teams like their linebackers 6-foot–2 or taller, so I held my breath when he gave my official height. They measured us in our bare feet. I wanted to rise up on my toes to give myself a little extra, but they acted like drill sergeants in making sure we didn't cheat even a little. When he got ready to read my height to the room, I thought, *Please let the first number be 6. Please, let it be 6.* I barely made it. I came in at just under six feet, one inch.

After the physical exam, the mental games started. Teams asked all sorts of strange questions to see how I'd react under pressure and to find out my values and motivations. To me, their questions seemed like psycho-babble. "Which would you rather be, a cat or a dog?" I told one team, "Look, I don't want to answer any of these stupid questions. Just tell me about your defense and how you run it so we can tell if I fit your system." I probably didn't score very high in any of those interviews.

I much preferred the physical testing, the drills and strength tests that came next. I knew players could soar up the draft board or fall off the face of the earth, depending on how they did in those areas. I felt some pressure to perform, but I didn't let it get to me. Cris Carter had come back to campus after playing his rookie year in the NFL, and he told me, "You have nothing to worry about. You know you can play, so don't get caught up in what people say." When I heard that, I relaxed, but I still wanted to do well at everything. The night before the testing, I magnified the importance of it so much I even gave myself a pep talk in my hotel room: "This is what you've waited your whole life for. Don't screw this up." Deep inside, I knew I wouldn't go out there and fall on my face. I wouldn't trip over my own feet. I hadn't trained to fail. Under pressure, I always had been able to perform. I knew that I had worked hard. I just had to trust my abilities. I'd never failed to answer the bell. Why would this be any different?

It wasn't. I didn't blow any of the tests the next day. My forty-yard dash time of 4.86 fell a little short of what the scouts wanted. I knew that would hurt me some, because they obsess over a linebacker's straight-line speed for forty yards. Fortunately, I had the fastest twenty-yard shuttle time among all the inside linebackers at the Combine. I believed that going back and forth, five yards at a time, and bending down to touch a line on the ground with every change of direction fit more in line with the kind of skills a linebacker needed to play in the NFL.

What *I* thought didn't matter, of course. You won't find any bigger egos than among pro coaches, whether head coaches or assistant coaches. If they take a liking to you, they believe they can coach you better than you've ever been coached before, and they believe they can get you to play better than you've ever played. They'll take a guy in the first round, despite a mediocre college career, if they fall in love with his measurables—his height, weight, speed, etc. I knew I wouldn't wow any scouts with how I looked in my underwear or how I ran, but I also knew I could play football. I just wanted someone to give me a chance to hit somebody.

It didn't help that I prepared to enter the NFL at a time when 3–4 defenses became the trend throughout the league. Back in the days of four linemen and three linebackers, defenses relied on middle line-backers like Dick Butkus and Ray Nitschke to make the majority of big plays. But when the preference shifted toward three linemen and four linebackers, every team started looking for pass-rushing outside linebackers, like Lawrence Taylor. Inside linebackers, like me, typi-cally played first and second downs and often came out of the game for an extra defensive back on passing downs. If you're not on the field for every play, you're less valuable. And if you're less valuable, they draft you lower and pay you less.

NFL types delight in tearing people down. They find every fault a player has, and if he doesn't have any faults, they'll invent some. They didn't need to search for my faults. They stuck the label "short and slow" on me. I had plenty of warts, including my refusal to answer whether I'd prefer being a cat or a dog. I clearly didn't fit their notion of the prototype computer printout linebacker. Mel Kiper Jr., the draft expert on ESPN, said I would make "a solid fourth- to sixth-round selection."

I consoled myself by remembering what Cris told me about his cer-tainty that I could play in the NFL, that I had nothing to worry about. But for a guy who dreamed his whole life of playing in the NFL, for a guy who had a bumper sticker over the bed in his college apartment that said, "Play in the NFL," it damaged my confidence to hear scouts talk more about my faults than my strengths.

I did have one thing in my favor—this new gizmo called "The Box." A NASA engineer designed it to help NFL teams measure players' agility in distances shorter than forty yards. The Box cost about $10,000, so not everyone had one. Cincinnati and Tampa put me through it, but neither made any promises. Houston said what I wanted to hear. Its head coach, Jerry Glanville, told me on my visit to their facility, "Chris, if you're there in the first round, we're taking you." I knew about the significant difference in money between a first-round pick and a second-round pick. That didn't concern me much, although I knew if I didn't get first-round money, I'd never recoup the money lost. My obsession with being a first-round pick didn't involve money; it was a matter of ego. It would humble me greatly to fall out of the first round.

Draft day—Saturday, April 24, 1988—finally arrived. I watched it at home in Canton with my mom and dad. I knew I wouldn't go in the Top Ten picks, but I still decided to watch the ESPN coverage from the very start. I hoped to go anywhere between fifteen and twenty-seven.

Instead, my teammate, Eric Kumerow, went to Miami at No. 16. No one expected Eric to be the first Ohio State player—particularly the first Ohio State *linebacker*—taken. I understood the choice. Miami didn't need me. They had drafted John Offerdahl at inside linebacker the year before, and he had a great rookie year. But it really ticked me off when Houston's turn came at twenty-two, and it picked Lorenzo White, a running back from Michigan State. The year before, Houston had chosen Alonzo Highsmith, a running back from Miami, in the first round. Houston also had Allen Pinkett, another pretty good running back, on its roster. In my not-very-humble opinion, Houston didn't need another running back.

The longer the first round continued, and the longer I didn't get picked, the more frustrated I became. I had waited long enough.

I stalked out of the family room and went upstairs to watch on the little black-and-white TV in Rick's room. Of course, TVs work better if you don't smash them against the wall, which I did shortly after walking into the room. I spent the next hour brooding … until Detroit took me with the second pick of the second round. Finally, I could be happy.

Just like a spoiled brat.

CHAPTER 10

REACHING THE DREAM

IT TOOK ME ABOUT TWO SECONDS TO GET OVER THE DILEMMA OF being an Ohio State guy drafted to play professional football for the Detroit Lions. The idea of *Michigan? Me, play in Michigan?* didn't bother me at all. I stood on the threshold of achieving my lifelong dream of becoming an NFL linebacker. I'd never put any restrictions on the team, city, or state where that had to happen. If the Lions wanted me, then I wanted them. I committed everything I had to showing them I belonged at that level.

During the entire run-up to the draft, I had only one brief conversation with anyone from Detroit. One of its scouts, Ron Hughes, walked past me in the Ohio State weight room one day and said, "Chris, if you're there in the second round, we're taking you." I thought, *Yeah, great.* I figured I wouldn't be available in the second round. But now that every team had passed over me in the first round, I became more determined than ever.

My brother, Rick, graduated from Southern Illinois in the spring of 1987 and tried out for the San Diego Chargers that fall, but they cut him. He signed with the Lions before the 1988 draft, so once they drafted me, I went with Rick to the Lions' off-season conditioning program at Oakland University in Michigan. We stayed together in a tiny dorm room with no air conditioning. It got so hot that summer, we slept on the tile floor of the room, trying to stay cool.

Growing up, Rick and I had shared a room from the time I could first remember until we moved into a bigger house when I entered the fifth grade. Being in that Oakland dorm together brought back all those old childhood memories. It also reenergized our brotherly competitiveness. We fought over what to watch on the three channels we could get on the black-and-white TV. We fought over who could eat the most for lunch every day at this little hot dog place called Coney Island.

Once the Lions' off-season workouts ended, I went back to Massillon to spend the summer with Stef and get ready for training camp. I couldn't imagine spending my life with anyone else, since I had never seriously dated anyone but Stef. One night we had a conversation about the direction of our relationship. I had to think about that, because things always had seemed so natural and unforced between us that I just assumed we would always be together. About a week later, just before I had to leave for Detroit, I woke up one morning and said to my mom, "I think I'm going to ask Stef to marry me today."

Mom said, "What?"

I just said, "Yep, this is it." So, I got in the car and drove to the mall and bought an engagement ring.

I went over to Stef's house to talk to her mom, Myra, and asked permission to marry her daughter. Stef and I already had a date planned to play miniature golf that night. When we reached the eighteenth hole, I asked her to go back to the seventeenth hole and look for my car keys. Of course, I had the keys with me all along. I wanted to distract her so I could hide the ring in the cup. Stef didn't suspect anything until she putted out, then she reached for her ball and found the ring box. It left her speechless. I walked her over to a picnic table, held her hand, and asked, "Will you marry me?"

Stef didn't say anything at first, probably because I had really surprised her. Finally she said, "Yes."

We returned to her house, and Myra and Stef started planning our wedding right then and there. By the time I left around midnight, we had set the date, selected the church, planned the menu, and hammered out most of the guest list. I went home thinking, *Gee, I don't know if I was quite ready for all that.* Still, I loved knowing that we would start spending the rest of our lives together after Stef finished her senior year at Ohio State and I finished my first year in the NFL.

STEF AND CHRIS

Chris's senior prom
Massillon Washington High School, 1984

STEF ON HER DAD'S SHOULDERS

Richard Belcher, her dad

SONNY SPIELMAN FEEDING CHRIS

Chris at about age two; getting some early protein

STEF IN CHEERLEADING OUTFIT

freshman year at Jackson High School

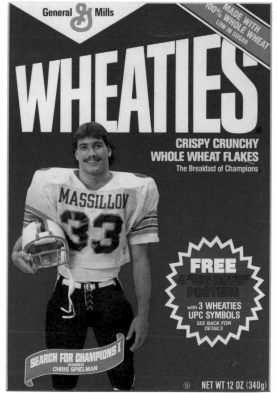

WHEATIES BOX

1983

STEF AND 36 JERSEY

in front of Christmas tree—
before the 1987 Cotton Bowl,
after the 1986 season

OHIO STATE

Jeff Uhlenhake, Chris, Frank Hoak, and
Tom Tupa at training camp, 1987

CHRIS AND STEF

graduating college, June 1989

WEDDING DAY

walking down the aisle in Canton, June 24, 1989

STEF AND CHRIS

during his rookie year in
Detroit, 1988

STEFANIE ON THE HALL OF FAME COURT

Pro Football Hall of Fame
ceremonies, 1984
(the year Paul Hornung
was inducted)

STEFANIE

modeling in Greece, 1990

CHRIS HOLDING MADDIE

Maddie less than a year old, 1995

FIRST DAY CHRIS WENT TO BUFFALO

Chris pictured in locker stall with Noah (four months) and
Maddie (two) after signing with the Bills as a free agent

HALL OF FAME GAME IN CANTON

during comeback with Browns, Fawcett Stadium, with
Maddie, Chris, Noah, and Stef, 1999

CHRIS AND STEF ON OPRAH

after Chris took year off from NFL, 1999

MADDIE AND NOAH

walking hand in hand at a Race for the Cure in
Columbus (Maddie, six; Noah, four)

BRINGING AUDREY HOME

July 2002

photo by Amy Parrish

RACE FOR THE CURE

Stef in pink survivor shirt, with Chris
and all four kids

SUE, MYRA, AND STEF

Stefanie's Champions Luncheon, 2007
photo by Greg Miller

FIRST BUCKEYE CRUISE FOR CANCER

Macy is sleeping on Chris and Audrey is
sleeping on Stefanie

THE SPIELMANS

jumping on trampoline

photo by Amy Parrish

STEF

riding the three-wheeler that Sue
borrowed for Myra, summer 2009

WINTER OLYMPICS

Stef carrying the Olympic torch
through the streets of Columbus,
January 2001

COLLEGE FOOTBALL HALL OF FAME

Stef celebrating Chris's recognition for College Football
Hall of Fame on the field in Ohio Stadium, with the
family and Archie Griffin, September 2009

NOAH THE NIGHT OF *HIGH SCHOOL MUSICAL*

Jones Middle School Auditorium, November 7, 2009

ALL THE KIDS WITH STEF

2009

In July, Rick and I returned to Oakland University for a mini-camp the Lions held for rookies and free agents, just before the team's veterans reported. I pulled a hamstring and had to sit out a week, which left Rick as the only middle linebacker. He had to take all the practice repetitions in all the scrimmages. That gave him a ton of chances to impress the coaches, but it also pushed him to the limit physically. I couldn't do much more than watch until my hamstring healed.

One day, while I sat on the bus that took us from the dorms to the practice field, I saw this big dude get on and walk down the aisle right toward me. I recognized the guy immediately: Eric Andolsek, the guy I had exchanged blows with before the coin toss down at LSU my senior year at Ohio State. The Lions chose Eric in the fifth round of the draft that spring. He came up to me with this big smile and said, "Hey, Chris, how you doing?" I didn't know what to think. I didn't want to fight him on the bus. But instead of taking a swing at me, he plopped down in the seat next to me and we ended up hitting it off pretty well.

The veterans, however, took an immediate dislike to me once training camp started. All veterans treat rookies like second-class citizens, but their problem with me went beyond the normal hazing given to the new guys. The veterans didn't like me because of how hard I practiced. They wanted to take it slow and ease back into football shape after taking six months off. As an unproven, first-year guy with a chip on my shoulder from getting passed over in the first round of the draft, I tried blowing up anyone in my way, even before we put on the pads. A few guys took me aside and told me to slow down. When I didn't, they started yelling at me, things like "Pontiac All-American," since we played our home games at the Pontiac Silverdome. Their taunts just made me push harder. I had my way of doing things that had earned me the opportunity to play in the NFL, so I wouldn't back off. When I crossed the lines, I went all out. I refused to slow down.

My hamstring injury from rookie camp flared up a few weeks into training camp, but I believed that once it healed, the middle linebacker spot would be mine for a long time. My competition consisted of Sheldon White, the guy who started the year before, and

Paul Butcher, a special-teams guy. Detroit drafted me to take over at middle linebacker, and everyone knew it.

We went to Cleveland for our first preseason game, and I played horribly. I hadn't practiced much because of my hamstring injury, so they held me out until the second half. I didn't make a single play all night. I knew I didn't play well, which earned me a severe ripping in our film session the next day. Darryl Rogers, the head coach, called me out in front of the entire team. "Spielman? Where's Spielman? You looked like a blind dog in a butcher shop out there. Why did we draft you? You're terrible."

Mike Murphy, our linebackers coach, told me later that week I would start the second preseason game against Seattle. "We're giving you your shot," he said. "Let's see what you can do." I realized early on in training camp that the adjustment from Ohio State to the NFL would be much harder than the adjustment from Massillon to OSU. Trying to cover a back out of the backfield, watching an offensive line work in perfect harmony, seeing linemen come off the ball with speed I never thought possible in someone that big—all of that really opened my eyes.

You can't simulate those things in practice, so I hoped that once I had a game under my belt, I would adjust. To make sure, I had a pep talk with myself before that Seattle game. It followed pretty much the same theme as my pep talk the night before my workout at the NFL Scouting Combine in February: "This is what you've been waiting for your whole life. Go do what you do. Don't screw it up." I played that whole game and did well, which put me back on schedule to start as a rookie.

I hoped Rick also would make the opening day roster. He and I had sat in meetings together, practiced together … I loved living my dream with him right there beside me. Then, on the day of the last cuts of training camp, I went into a team meeting and couldn't find Rick. I knew right then that they'd cut him. I understood his disappointment. If that had happened to me, I'd want everyone to leave me alone for a while. I gave him some space and didn't try to talk to him for about a week.

Rick had been cut two years in a row. A lot of guys hang on in that situation, even though getting cut in back-to-back years usually means the end of an NFL dream. Rick didn't try to hang on. Instead, he returned to school for his master's degree and started pursuing the path that would take him to a scouting job with the league and eventually to the general manager's job with the Minnesota Vikings.

I ended up starting every game that season, led the team in tackles, and won NFC defensive rookie-of-the-year. We finished 4–12, though, which really frustrated me. Although we had a subpar season at Ohio State the year before, I'd never lost as often in my football career as our twelve losses that first season in Detroit. As much as I hated losing, I hated it even more when *I* caused us to lose, like I did against Chicago in our next-to-last game of the regular season.

The Bears already had clinched the division, but we had a 12–10 lead late in the fourth quarter. If we stopped them one more time, we would win. Jim Harbaugh, the quarterback from Michigan who had "guaranteed" a win over Ohio State my junior year, took some snaps while they rested their starters for the playoffs.

Harbaugh floated a pass out into the flat, which I saw coming the whole way. I got both hands on it and should have pulled it in for an easy game-clinching interception. But when I hit the ground, the ball popped out. After that, Chicago drove down and kicked the winning field goal. We lost, 13–12. I knew I had lost the game for us.

In the locker room afterward, some of my teammates came up and tried to make me feel better. "It's OK, Chris. We wouldn't have been that close without you." Yeah, whatever. I knew that my fifteen tackles meant nothing. If I had made that play, we would have won, pure and simple. I didn't catch the ball and we lost; therefore, I lost the game.

When I went home to Massillon that summer, I couldn't believe what I saw hanging in my dad's house—a giant photo of me sprawled on my knees in Soldier Field, arms extended, looking up in frustration after dropping that interception.

"What are you doing with that?" I asked my dad. "Of all the pictures you could have, why do you have *that* picture on your wall?"

"I like the shot," he answered. "Look at it. It captures the emotion."

"You want to see some emotion?" I said. "I'll show you some emotion." I rammed my fist right through the photograph and the frame. Then I took them out in the backyard and burned them.

The frustration of my rookie year aside, being an NFL player lived up to all my expectations. I felt honored and privileged to wear the uniform. I wore Lions' gear like a school kid. T-shirts, hats, jackets ... anything with Lions on it, I wore it. I'd "made it" as an NFL player, and I let everybody know it.

Eric Andolsek and I ended up getting an apartment together. He even bought the Lions coat, like the one Eddie Murphy wore in the movie *Beverly Hills Cop*. I borrowed it and wore it a few times. Not many people get to the NFL, so my first year, I took every opportunity to show off my pride in achieving that goal.

Both Eric and I planned on getting married in the off-season, so neither of us had any interest in the nightclub scene. If Stef or Eric's fiancée came to town, we would go out to dinner. But otherwise, I understood what it meant to play in the NFL and how much hard work it took to get there. I didn't allow anything to get in my way and screw that up. I'd occasionally hear someone on the radio refer to some player and say, "He hits like an NFL linebacker." I thought, *That's me. I'm an NFL linebacker*. It made me feel good. *Really* good.

Following my rookie year, I returned to Ohio State for the winter and spring quarters to finish my degree in recreation education. Stef also graduated that June. We got married two weeks later and moved to Detroit to start our life together.

One of the best things we did was get involved in our team Bible study. Dave Wilson, the Lions' chaplain, led the discussions and wound up making a huge impact on us. Stef and I began noticing that the more we worked to put God first in our lives, the more our love for each other grew. Before that, I thought, *I could never love anything more than I love my wife*.

I began to understand that my faith called me to have a growing relationship with Christ, which meant I could incorporate the attitudes and behavior He spoke about in the Bible into my own approach toward life. I realize that might seem incompatible with my job as a professional football player because I had to be tough, physical, and, at times, nasty with my opponents. Yet at the same time, I noticed that single-minded focus—one of my greatest attributes—could characterize godly men. While God would have to channel that focus, He used football to hone it.

I can't say I always lived or spoke perfectly in those days. But I realized that my duty as a Christian called me to live that way *all* the time, not just when convenient. I discovered the Bible has a lot to say about love, marriage, and putting others ahead of yourself, and the more I put those things into practice, the more my love for Stef grew —beyond anything I had ever imagined.

In some respects, we were an unlikely couple. Stef had it so together; she didn't fit the profile of someone likely to fall for a professional athlete. A lot of athletes' wives get their identity from their husband's job or the status that goes with it. My career meant something to Stef only because she knew how much importance I placed on being in the NFL. She shared my joy in reaching that goal, but she didn't need my fame to feel good about herself. She had a dynamic personality of her own. She didn't just blindly follow me; she was a leader in her own right. While her beauty opened doors for her as a professional model and host of her own TV show in Detroit, Stef was far from some empty-headed trophy wife who latched onto an NFL player so she could ride the financial gravy train.

She had a depth to her that allowed her to see qualities in me beyond just my obsession with football. My drive to excel made me different from other guys in high school. I knew what I wanted and I committed everything to it. When we first met, I had a singular focus that appealed to her. She loved my ability to focus and my determination to accomplish whatever I set out to do. In fact, in a videotape she made for our kids once she knew she didn't have long to live, she spoke of those qualities in me that she loved. "This is who your dad is," she said. "This is why I loved him. This is what helped him to get through the situation with me." While I lacked the complete self-confidence that she had, I did have a purpose that drove me, and I know that attracted her.

One of the really cool things, and one of the reasons I loved her, was that our relationship lacked any jealousy. In a lot of ways, Stef behaved like a guy. She didn't like to talk on the phone, and neither did I. She would tell me exactly how she felt, and she didn't take offense when I did the same. Stef could be just as blunt as I was, not only in our conversations but when she spoke to others. One time, Stef went jogging with one of her best friends, our next-door neighbor Claire Hamilton. Claire liked to talk while she ran. Stef didn't. Claire started chatting away during the first couple of hundred yards. Stef turned to her and said, "Claire, I love you. But seriously, are you planning to talk the whole way? Because if you are, I'm outta here." And off she went.

That sounds like something I would have said, which made us perfect for each other.

Neither of us ever had to worry about whether we said something "the right way." We never guessed with each other. I could tell her, "I'm not going to Europe on vacation. I'm not getting on a plane for eight hours. The continental United States is perfect. There must be some place we can go in the continental United States. I don't want to go to Europe. I have no interest in Europe." When I spoke like that, I didn't hurt her feelings. I didn't have to worry, "How do I say this?" I just said it. "I'm not going. You can go. Grab some friends and go."

So the first year of our marriage, Stef modeled in Greece for six months. She took her mom and they traveled all over. They had a great time. Stef didn't hold a grudge against me for not going, and I didn't blame her for leaving me in Detroit. I didn't want to ever hold her back. I didn't want my achieving my dreams to keep her from achieving her dreams.

CHAPTER 11

SEARCHING FOR SUCCESS

WHILE STEF MODELED IN GREECE AND I LIVED ALONE IN OUR HOME in Detroit, the Lions embarked on a new era in my second season with the team in 1989. In April, the Lions drafted Barry Sanders, a Heisman Trophy winner, which gave us great optimism for our first full season under Wayne Fontes as head coach. We had a tradition in camp to watch the NFL Films highlight video from the year before. But instead of playing the highlight film for the 4–12 Detroit Lions of 1988, Wayne showed a highlight film of Barry Sanders in college at Oklahoma State. When it ended, we stood up and cheered. We knew we had something in Barry that no one else had.

Just as Coach Bruce had enforced a hands-off rule on Cris Carter, so Wayne had a hands-off rule on Barry because of his importance to our team. But just like at Ohio State, I couldn't resist. One day Barry came through the hole, running hard, and I just had to see what it felt like to hit him. It felt like I had rammed my head into a tree. His legs felt like rocks. It jarred my teeth when I hit him. When Wayne saw the hit, he came over to talk to me. He always smoked a cigar at practice, and he had this way of talking to everyone as if they were his best friend. "Chris," he said, "man, you know I love you to death. We go way back. We're both Canton boys. But if you hit Barry again, your ass will be on a bus out of here."

I played with Barry for seven seasons, and nobody in the league compared to him. He ranks in my book as the best pure runner ever. Barry blew up my theory that achieving greatness requires a certain passion for the game. He didn't put the same emphasis on the sport that I did, but he was still the best at what he did. I don't know if he took the wins and losses to heart like the rest of us. He told me once, "It's a game, Chris." If anyone else had said that to me, I might have punched him. To me, that would have indicated a lack of commitment, something that would have caused me to think less of him as a player. But Barry's performance stood out so far above everyone else that I couldn't question him. I stood in awe of what he could do. Whatever his attitude, when he stepped between the lines, he was fantastic. His perspective on football as just a game certainly didn't affect his efforts in practice or in games. His focus never wavered. He never got high and he never got low. He was just plain great.

Man, could he run.

My passion for football, off the chart since my first organized game at nine years old, went absolutely out of sight after getting to the NFL. Winning became an obsession. I wanted to win a Super Bowl so badly I considered anything short of that a complete failure. I did anything I could if I thought it would give me the slightest edge over my competition. I tried to arrive at the facility before any other player. I waited to leave until everyone else went home. No one studied more film than I did. I tried to bring an element of training to everything I did, like when I'd shuffle sideways up the stairs to our bedroom to work on my lateral mobility. I dreamed up things that no one else would do just to give myself an edge. I don't know if those things actually gave me that edge, but in my mind they did, so that made them worthwhile.

One of my rituals took place before training camp every year. After getting in my running at Rochester High School, I'd put on a plastic suit, get in my truck, roll the windows up, and turn the heater on full blast. I'd drive around with my mouth full of chewing tobacco and see how long I could last without spitting. I'd just swallow the tobacco juice and fight the urge to puke. It tested me mentally to see how long I could go without throwing up. It helped me simulate playing through distractions and taught me to focus. I think I lasted an hour and twenty-nine minutes one time. When I finished, I'd grab a bottle of water and try to rehydrate.

I knew other guys didn't do those kinds of things. Maybe I didn't need to do them either, but I thought I did. To *not* do them, I believed, would have been to sell the game short. And playing in the NFL meant too much to me to ever sell the game short.

Some of my shenanigans had no real purpose. They just exposed runaway competitiveness among testosterone-fueled teammates. For instance, we had an indoor jet pool in our training room. Marc Spindler, Ken Dalifor, and I would go in there, and one of us would put on goggles and a snorkel and go under so he could watch and referee. The other two guys would take turns going under, holding our eyes open while looking into the jets, just to see how long we could last without blinking.

Even with a weapon like Barry Sanders, it took three years before we finally made the playoffs. I don't know if I've ever been around a team as close as that one in 1991. A lot of the players and their wives got together throughout the week for game nights. We'd sit around and play Pictionary or Scruples. Afterward, instead of going to a nice restaurant, we'd have pizza and wings. You would think that twenty-something couples would have preferred to go clubbing. Instead, we did things that high school or college students might do. That closeness really helped us late in the year when one of our offensive linemen, Mike Utley, suffered an injury that left him paralyzed.

I saw Mike go down on the play. As he lay on the field, I watched the replay on the big screen. Right away I could see the severity of Mike's injury. He had tried to cut-block the defensive lineman, which meant at the snap Mike dove toward his lower legs. The lineman, doing what he could to protect himself, pushed away while pushing Mike down. Mike landed with the crown of his helmet hitting the ground, and that pushed his chin into his chest.

As they carted him off the field, he gave a thumbs-up to the crowd. It amazed me that a guy in that condition could say, "Hey, don't worry about me. I'll be all right." That thumbs-up became a rallying cry for us. Mike's spirit and optimism, even in the hospital that night, lifted us all and became the inspiration for us reaching the NFC championship game, where we lost to the Washington Redskins. Mike's injury, and how he handled it, galvanized us emotionally.

I really admired Mike's competitiveness. He didn't fit the mold of the classic NFL offensive lineman. He had a difficult time bench-pressing, so he didn't look very strong. But when he played, he had a nasty temperament that made him a beast to deal with.

Of all my thoughts of Mike as a player, one remains burned in my memory. The Lions had drafted Herman Moore, a wide receiver out of Virginia, in the first round. He caught a pass in one of our pre-season games and went down to avoid taking a hit. The next thing I saw was big No. 60 sprinting in a full gallop down the field. It was Mike. He picked Herman up, got in his face, and pointed to the end zone. In other words, "Rookie, don't you dare give up like that. When you catch the ball, give everything you have to score a touchdown." I thought, *That's the attitude you win with.*

I'll never forget that play. I loved it. I loved everything about it. Mike Utley had the attitude necessary to play the game the right way. He had it in practice. He had it in the preseason. He had it in the regular season. Out on that field, I knew I could trust Mike Utley.

That off-season in June, Stef and I took a cruise to Puerto Rico. One night at dinner on board ship, someone came up to me and said, "Mr. Spielman, you have an emergency telephone call from Chuck Schmidt of the Detroit Lions." I didn't know what to think about get-ting that kind of call from our general manager. I wondered if they'd made a trade; I had no real idea.

When I picked up the phone, Chuck said, "Chris, Eric Andolsek died tonight." A truck driver, high on cocaine, swerved off the road and hit Eric while he stood near the highway, weed-whacking the grass in his front yard. Eric never heard the truck coming because of the weed-whacker's engine noise.

I could see the accident in my mind. A few years before, I had vis-ited Eric in Thibodeaux, Louisiana. Eric, his mom, his brother, and his sister all lived in a row in four houses. The truck hit him as he stood near the mailbox, slamming him a couple hundred feet over his brother's yard and into his sister's yard. He never had a chance.

Stef and I left the ship immediately and went straight to Louisi-ana for the funeral. I gave the eulogy. Eric's wife, Cheryl, had asked me to do it. She and Stef had become good friends during our years in Detroit. We attended their wedding and they came to ours. Eric even worked out with me in Canton on my wedding day. We had a natural bond as two young guys who both loved football. I spoke at the funeral about the difficulty of losing someone in the prime of life. "But if you were God," I said, "wouldn't you want Eric on your team?"

Given what had happened to both Eric and to Mike, our team lacked its normal enthusiasm when training camp began in 1992. We carried a lot of emotional baggage into that season, and we played horribly. We really underperformed after reaching the NFC championship game the year before.

Stef got pregnant with Maddie during the 1993 season, which helped soften some of my rough edges. We always planned on Stef becoming a full-time mom when we started our family. God had blessed us with the financial ability for one of us to stay home. Stef wanted to do that, or she wouldn't have married me. That was just another instance of us knowing where we stood with each other.

We didn't have a lot of fights between us. When we did disagree, I sometimes let my linebacker mentality take over. I told her once, "I'll be down in the basement watching sports. Come down when you're done being mad." Another time I said, "Why don't you put all your ideas on how I can be a better husband into a suggestion box, and I'll read them when I get time." I definitely had a Neanderthal side, and a lot of people thought that side defined me. Stef saw through all that rough exterior and wound up the one and only person who really knew me.

Maddie was born in March 1994, and Noah came along two years later. Having children deepened the love in our marriage. It also increased the importance for me to learn what the Bible required of me not just as a husband, but also as a father. When I found out the Bible mandated that I become the spiritual leader in our home, I began to take on that role. I just tried to follow the playbook.

Stef accepted me in that role, but she also knew the Bible doesn't teach that women are inferior to men spiritually. We understood that God designed marriage as a true partnership, so we leaned on each other. Early in our marriage, Stef did a much better job than I did of putting God first in her life. I *wanted* to do that. I knew I *should* do that. But during my playing days, trying to be the best and winning a Super Bowl consumed me.

We made the playoffs in 1993, 1994, and 1995, but never got out of the first round. I tore the pectoral muscle in my right arm in the first game of the '95 season against the Steelers when I tried to tackle Jerome Bettis. Dermontti Dawson, their center, slammed me in my back at the same time, which ripped my pec and locked it, with my fist pointing up at a 90-degree angle. I returned to the huddle and said to Marc Spindler, "Punch my arm down." When he did, my pec unlocked so I could play another snap. For the rest of the game, I had Marc push my arm down between plays.

I ended up playing that way for the rest of the season. Before every game, they took a needle and drained the blood out of this ball that had formed under my arm. I didn't have full strength in the muscle, but I got by. It wound up not mattering much, because Philadelphia smoked us in the playoffs.

When a team loses in the first round three straight years, changes are bound to happen. So it didn't surprise me that the Lions made no effort to re-sign me. It bothered me a little that I got no explanation, but they obviously wanted to go in a different direction. That's how I became a free agent.

Buffalo, the New York Giants, and Green Bay all made offers. I wanted to go where I could win. Buffalo had played in four straight Super Bowls in the '90s. The Bills had a veteran team with a hole at my position. I met their coach, Marv Levy, and loved him, so it just felt right to go there.

I slid into the middle linebacker spot vacated when Cornelius Bennett signed with Atlanta. We went 10–6 and made the playoffs, but lost at home to Jacksonville on a field goal. I set a team record with 206 tackles, so I thought I'd justified their faith in signing me. They gave me a new contract after the season that added another year to my deal, along with another signing bonus. That helped make up for some of the money I lost when I fell into the second round of the draft.

Jim Kelly retired after that season, so in 1997 Todd Collins became our quarterback. We started slow, going 3–3 heading into a Monday night game at Indianapolis, where that life-altering question—"Chris, what is your purpose in life?"—came into my mind. That signaled the first hint of the mammoth changes about to hit my life, Stef's life, and our life as a family.

Throughout my NFL career, I kept a sign in my locker that read, "Super Bowl champs, the only thing that matters." I had an obsession with being the best, being on the best, and being part of the best. That's how I defined myself, first and foremost. I loved my wife and I loved my children and I loved God. Although I had a personal relationship with Christ at that time, it didn't always rank at the top of my list. Some days it fell from 1A to 1B or 1C. Some days it dropped to No. 2 or even No. 3.

The longer my NFL career lasted, once I could see the end on the horizon, I became harder and harder on myself and intolerant of my mistakes on the field. Stef said to me once, "I've never seen anyone live their dream and be so unhappy." As I fought to hold on, I imposed more conditions, more rules, more stipulations, more work, more focus, more *anything* to keep playing at the level I demanded of myself.

Looking back, I realize I failed to walk daily with Christ when I played. I certainly thought about God and Jesus, but sometimes my faith took a backseat. I knew what I believed and why I believed it. I understood that God's grace, through Christ's death on the cross, gave me the free gift of salvation. But other things demanded my time and attention, so I prioritized: family, football, faith—in that order.

Before long, those priorities got rearranged in a big way.

CHAPTER 12

FINDING A NEW PURPOSE

STEFANIE'S BREAST CANCER DIAGNOSIS IN JULY 1998, THE CHEMO-
therapy treatments that followed, and my decision to take a one-year
leave from the NFL to care for her shoved football farther down my
priority list than ever before. Intellectually, I always knew the sport
didn't rank ahead of my wife or my children. Yet it was one thing to
know in my head, and another to react with my heart and prove that
the code I professed to live by was more than empty words.

After Stef got sick, the importance of serving God, community,
and family took precedence over football in my personal pecking
order. Stef always had her priorities ordered more sensibly than I did,
and now she had more influence because of the greater challenge
in front of her. She embraced that challenge by serving as the face
of breast cancer in Columbus, once the Stefanie Spielman Fund for
Breast Cancer Research took shape. That process began right after
Stef's mastectomy. We received a call from a public relations firm
that represented a local supermarket chain, Big Bear. They said they
wanted to start a fund in Stefanie's honor at the Arthur G. James Cancer Hospital and Solove Research Institute on the Ohio State campus.

Stef quickly realized the platform she had and the difference she
could make. The timing concerned me because I thought Stef needed
to devote all her strength to getting better. But she felt strongly that
we couldn't turn down the opportunity, and so we agreed. She saw it
as an avenue God had provided for us to put our faith into action and
serve others. Stef believed that by going public with her battle, she
could inspire those with the disease to fight harder. She also hoped

to prompt those who didn't have breast cancer to contribute research dollars toward finding a cure.

The goals for the fund meshed with our belief system and our mentality. As we assessed Stef's situation, we saw we had several options. We could hide in the corner, fold, and quit, or we could punch back. Stef felt just as inclined to fight as I did. She also wanted to make a difference, because talking to other women who had preceded her in this fight really inspired her. She understood that with the notoriety we had—because of my Ohio State and NFL careers, the corporate support behind us, and the world-class cancer hospital just five miles from our house—we had a unique opportunity. We could do more than just motivate people. We could actually save lives. Both of us viewed that possibility as an awesome responsibility that we just couldn't turn down.

On September 3, 1998, we announced the formation of the fund and set a goal of raising $250,000 by the end of the year. Ralph Wilson, the owner of the Bills, sent a $10,000 check the first month, and things just snowballed from there. Big Bear offered people the chance to purchase a paper football cutout for $1 at checkout, with that amount going to Stef's Fund. It encouraged us tremendously to drive around Columbus during chemo and see the windows of every Big Bear store covered with little paper footballs and people's signatures on them. In Central Ohio alone, Big Bear raised $137,450 directly from the sale of those paper footballs—one customer and one dollar at a time. Other donations totaling $131,000 came directly to The James.

Because of her background as a fashion model and because she had hosted her own television show in Detroit, Stef knew how to handle the spotlight. She personalized breast cancer for a lot of people. They saw a young, beautiful, active mom, someone who by her own words enjoyed "a fairy-tale life," threatened by the disease in the prime of her life. The fact that breast cancer could strike her, and therefore could attack anyone, really resonated with people.

Neither of us envisioned such an overwhelming response. We had no idea if it would take off, and certainly no clue it would spread like a brush fire. The fund hit more than $1 million in the first six months, and then just kept going. I believe God prompted people to embrace it as a reward for Stef responding to His call on her life. She never shied away from it. At a time when she needed her strength for her first round of chemo, she dove headlong into the demands of the fund.

Those responsibilities weighed on her sometimes, but she always saw the fund as something bigger than her own situation. It gave her an avenue to help others by inspiring them to cope with breast cancer, motivating them to get a mammogram or do a self-breast exam, or encouraging them to give to research.

The money rolled in from everywhere, including a bunch of grassroots community efforts. Little League tournaments, lemonade stands, bake sales, golf outings—no event and no contribution was too insignificant to matter. And it all added up quickly. The thing just took on a life of its own, which floored Stef and me.

For some reason, I think people always connected with me as a player. Maybe my attitude drew them in, or they identified with what I said in interviews, or maybe they just liked how I played. People seemed to view me as one of them. I gained a lot of notoriety as a high school player after being on the front of a Wheaties box, so most people knew about me when I decided to attend Ohio State. I made All-American as a junior and senior, which made me even more well-known because of OSU's large fan base. I made the Pro Bowl four times playing in blue-collar towns like Detroit, Buffalo, and Cleveland, so that brought some additional name recognition.

I think the fans in those cities liked me because I never drove fancy cars, lived in a fancy house, or did anything to suggest that I felt superior to them. When we lost a game, I showed my frustration by ranting about how I hated losing, how I stunk, or how our team stunk. I think those kinds of actions resonated with the fans. I was a regular guy, just like them. My job just happened to be playing football.

When cancer struck, those same fans could envision themselves in my situation: *Hey, this could happen to me. He's just like I am.*

The media made a big deal out of me skipping the 1998 season in Buffalo to help take care of Stef during her chemo. *USA Today,*

Esquire magazine, *Sports Illustrated*, and many others wrote about it. Stef and I appeared on *Oprah, Donnie & Marie, Good Morning America*, and a lot of other shows.

It made for a good story: an NFL player in the prime of his career taking a year off from the sport during his wife's breast cancer treatments. I tried to make the point in every interview that my job in the NFL gave us the financial blessing to allow me to quit for a while to stay at home. I found it strange that people saw it as some sort of noble gesture, when I knew any man with the means to do it would have made the same choice. I didn't think I deserved, nor did I want, any credit.

I understood why my decision surprised some guys in the NFL. They'd never seen a side of me other than my psycho football persona. I never showed anything but Football Chris at work. I didn't socialize much with my teammates outside the facility. Around them, they saw me focused on only one thing: "What do we have to do to win?" But having my wife miscarry a child and then finding out she had breast cancer turned my world upside down and radically changed my perspective. My single-minded focus would now get turned to more important matters.

Shortly after we made the decision to go public with Stef's diagnosis, one of the highest-ranking doctors at The James confided his fear to a friend of mine that Stef and I would never be able to put this battle down or get any separation from it. He didn't understand that she didn't *want* to put it down. She had this amazing clarity almost immediately, even from that night in the car on the way to the hospital for her very first appointment when she scolded me for questioning, "Why us?" She wrote in her journal and said in one of her first interviews, "I know there's a reason God gave me breast cancer, and now it's up to me to do something with it."

Stef drew tremendous motivation from women who wrote to say they'd found a lump after seeing her on the news or reading about her. She took so much satisfaction from hearing that someone else's cancer had been detected early enough because of something she said about doing a self-breast exam or getting a mammogram.

Of course, along with the good stories came some tough ones. Some of those who became dear friends didn't win their battle. We had to get used to that harsh reality, because there are no ties in the cancer world. There are only wins and losses—exhilarating wins and devastating losses.

Once Stef began to feel better after her first chemo in the spring of 1999, she took a more active role in the management of the fund with the people from The James. She spent hours returning emails from people who contacted her through the hospital's website. She believed her work had a worthwhile purpose. She had found her calling, and I enjoyed being her biggest cheerleader.

After my comeback with the Browns fell short, I knew I'd eventually have to find something to occupy my time. I always assumed I would become a coach after my playing days ended. I enjoyed every aspect of the game, not just playing it. I loved the strategy behind why certain things worked and why others didn't. My dad had coached high school football for more than forty years, and I saw the impact he made on his players—so coaching seemed like a sensible second career for me.

It made even more sense given how close I'd become to the guys around the Ohio State program. I had a great relationship with Dave Kennedy after working out under his supervision. I'd gotten to know John Cooper, the head coach, and some of his assistants very well. Guys like Luke Fickell, John Tenuta, and Fred Pagac, assistants on the defensive side, welcomed me into their meetings to watch film with them. Coach Cooper always hinted that I'd have a spot on his staff if I wanted it.

I also had a few options in the NFL. Several teams called during my first weeks at home to gauge my interest in getting involved with their franchises. But for some reason, despite all the things that pointed me toward coaching, I just didn't have a passion for it. That surprised me. Stef's recovery and how naturally our life at home returned to normal made leaving her and the kids for the long hours of coaching a very unattractive option.

This time, the transition away from football went a lot easier than it did the year before. Stef had completely recovered. At least, that's what we both believed. So far as we knew, she had beaten cancer forever. The previous year, when I decided not to play, I fought the urge to play again after healing from my neck surgery. Now I had no illusions about going back. My body wouldn't allow it. That made the transition easier, and so did the fact that I had no regrets. I had peace over how I approached every practice and every game. I could look at myself and know I'd given everything I had.

It didn't take long for me to realize that even though I had left the NFL behind, I still had a team and we had a big game to win. I joined that team led by the doctors, researchers, and fundraisers at The James. We resolved to beat cancer, the toughest opponent I'd ever faced. The similarities to football and the significance of the stakes —my wife's recovery—motivated me to help her raise awareness and research dollars. Stef teased me that she knew I had become fully committed when she saw me willingly wear pink—the color affiliated with breast cancer and its treatment.

I made a conscious effort to approach Stef's cancer battle differently than I did my football career. In one arena at least, I wanted to adopt a completely different mind-set than I had as a player. When we won a game in football, I never really celebrated, because I looked forward to the next game and the next challenge too much to enjoy whatever we had accomplished. I committed to bringing a different attitude to this new contest involving life and death. I'd never fully enjoyed my success in the NFL, and I didn't want to be like that anymore. I wanted to enjoy a freedom I never enjoyed as a player.

With cancer, I didn't want to obsess over "Is it back?" So if Stef had a clear scan, I tried hard not to immediately think, *When is the next scan?* I would give myself until about ten days out from the next scan before I thought about what it might show. I avoided looking at calendars or anything that might remind me of the date of her next scan. I tried to delay my anxiety as long as possible, because I knew my personality would trigger—just like it had in football—a nagging obsession. I would become consumed by that date, just like the games consumed me in the NFL. I didn't want that attitude to hold me prisoner anymore.

Over the next twelve years, as Stef applied herself to the fund and its mission, she transitioned into the role of being in the spotlight more than me. I became known as much for being her husband as for my football career. I loved watching her blossom and take center stage. The more times she battled through treatment and continued to fight, the more her profile grew and the greater her impact became. The courage she showed left an indelible impression on everyone. I used to think when I played that I saw some great examples of courage from my teammates or opponents. In fact, I didn't have a clue about courage until I watched Stef. She provided the best example I ever saw of someone leading by her actions, of standing up and being responsible and accountable when she didn't have to be.

Stef explained her motivation many times in many speeches: "I've always been the type of person to let other people know that everything is going to be OK. I wanted my family to know that Mom took a bad situation and made something good come from it." Stef grew so comfortable in front of people that she rarely spoke from notes. She developed a knack for tailoring her comments to a particular audience. A lot of times, she brought our kids along so they grew comfortable in the cancer world and with its harsh realities.

While we gladly served as the face of the fund, both of us wanted to make more of a personal impact on its growth. For the first few years, it felt like other people did the heavy lifting, while we received the praise for their hard work. We tried to come up with an idea to add to the bottom line that would also fit us as a couple.

The first Stefanie's Champions luncheon grew out of that brainstorming in April 2000. Instead of honoring people who had cancer, Champions honored those who offered support. Stef envisioned it as a way to take the focus off the patient and affirm the sacrifices that husbands, wives, family members, friends, and others made, so those stricken with cancer could concentrate on beating the disease. No one should have to go through such an ordeal alone. Those who cook, clean, schedule, organize, and take the patient to their appointments are essential too.

The best thing about Champions isn't the big financial contribution every year. It's the wave of inspiration that everyone rides after the event. The stories of the honorees and the love between them and the people they've cared for make the tears flow and the emotions swell. It would take an unfeeling heart not to be moved by the triumph that grows out of such tough circumstances.

A lot of charitable endeavors start strong and then fizzle out, but the fund just kept gaining momentum. Every dollar ever raised has gone directly to research. The fund falls under the OSU Foundation, which pays all the administrative costs, so donations can finance studies that lead to new drugs, new treatment regimens, new therapies, and other breakthroughs. We created a tumor bank so that doctors can study cancerous tissues in hopes of finding a cure more quickly. Some of Stef's treatments in later years didn't exist when doctors first diagnosed her.

The satisfaction of playing a role in efforts that help save or prolong a person's life goes miles beyond the significance of winning a football game. During my college career, I experienced the best of Ohio State athletically. But The James introduced Stef and me to a different world of committed people who want to make Ohio State the best in the world at treating and curing cancer. The more we got involved, the more that thrilled us.

Stef came up with the idea to take $25,000 from the fund each year to create the Patient Assistance Fund, which pays for wigs, groceries, cab fare, or whatever else people need to cope with the challenges brought on by treatment. She really enjoyed seeing that money applied to someone in dire need. One Christmas, she went with her friend Jennifer McDonald to a home where the mother's struggle with cancer made it impossible for her to provide gifts for her two daughters. Stef and Jen brought a Christmas tree, decorated the home, provided presents for the family, and gave the mother a camera so she could take pictures of their Christmas.

The mom grew very emotional and began crying. Stef bent down to comfort her in her wheelchair. "I'm not going to make it," the lady said. "I'm not going to make it." Stef hugged her, then looked her in the eye and attempted to reassure her. "You just have to have faith and believe," Stef said. "You have to have hope."

And with that, Stef reached into her coat and pulled out an ornament for the tree, inscribed with just a single word:

"Hope."

"It was," Jen said, "the most beautiful, touching thing I've ever seen."

CHAPTER 13

Don't Blame Macy

WHILE STEF FOUND HER CALLING WITH THE FUND AND WORKING AS an advocate for breast cancer issues, as an ex-player I found something even more cliché than landing a coaching job. IMG Broadcasting contacted me in the fall of 1999 and offered me an audition for a new show on the Fox Sports cable channels. I got the job working with Chris Myers, Jackie Slater, and my old coach in Buffalo, Marv Levy, on a program called *NFL Sunday Morning*. I flew to Los Angeles every Friday and returned on Sunday night, so I didn't spend much time away from the family.

During the week, I worked out at the Ohio State football facility and continued to build friendships with the coaches I spent so much time with the year before during Stef's chemotherapy. I sat in on meetings, talked strategy, and watched practice almost every day. So when a spot opened up on the staff after the 1999 season, Coach Cooper asked if I wanted to become a full-time assistant. Now I had a concrete offer from my alma mater and the temptation to do something I had dreamed about during my playing days at OSU. I told the *Columbus Dispatch* early in my senior year, "I want to come back here and coach 20 or 30 years and break Woody Hayes' record. I love Ohio State. I've had a taste of it as a player. What would be better than to come back and be the coach?"

Twelve years later, I still loved my alma mater—but I realized that I loved our new life even more. Stef had managed an amazing bounce-back. She felt almost as good as she did before her diagnosis. I got into golf and waterskiing. We did things as a couple, like traveling with friends, that I enjoyed too much to give up. Stef would have supported me had I chosen to coach at Ohio State, but it made her happy when I told her over breakfast that I planned to turn down Coach Cooper's offer. I didn't have a burning desire to become a college assistant coach. Working in television intrigued me. I wanted to see how far I could go in that field.

Shortly after making that decision, we got a big surprise when Stef became pregnant with our third child. We weren't trying to have more children, but we weren't not trying either. The previous time Stef became pregnant, she discovered the lump that led to her breast cancer diagnosis. This pregnancy didn't scare her. It thrilled her, because it meant her life had returned to normal. We wanted more children at the time of her first diagnosis, but she had miscarried. This new pregnancy convinced us Stef had fallen into that fortunate 70-to-80 percent share of women who, once diagnosed, get treatment and then never have a recurrence.

In the fall of 2000, Fox decided to jazz up the *NFL Sunday Morning* show by including Billy Ray Smith, Sean Jones, Bob Golic, and Jay Mohr, a comedian. They built an upper set for the original crew —me, Jackie Slater, Chris Myers, and Marv Levy—and a lower set, with couches, for the new guys. They encouraged us to roam back and forth in a setup that became the model for what evolved into *The Best Damn Sports Show Period*. Instead of a pure football show, we now had a sports/entertainment hybrid.

I didn't do a good job hiding my disdain for the new arrangement. A producer called me into a meeting one day and said, "Your look of disgust is not good for the show and what we're doing." I asked him what he wanted me to do. "We're not going to have you on the show anymore," he said. Basically, I got fired; but that ended up being the biggest break of my broadcasting career. Fox still had to pay me, so they put me on Big 12 football games for the last half of the year. Dave Lapham, who had played for the Cincinnati Bengals, did the analysis for those games. Dave could have been territorial about having me in the booth as a third guy, but instead he welcomed me with open arms and showed me the ropes.

Right after college football's regular season ended, the pressure started to build on Coach Cooper at Ohio State, like it did for any OSU coach who lost to Michigan. He probably would have survived, but the team also lost in the Outback Bowl after a week marked by some off-field player behavior issues. OSU fired him the morning after the game, on January 2. Right away, I got some phone calls from people who said, "Get your resume ready!" I hadn't given coaching any thought since turning down the offer to become an assistant almost a year earlier. But the chance to become the head coach of my alma mater tugged on me a lot more. I thought, *Why not? Why not take a shot?*

Stef encouraged me to put a plan together, so I met with my agent, Bret Adams, and together we mapped out a strategy. I had a fund-raising plan, a recruiting plan, a plan for the offense and defense I would run ... everything. I called some coaches around the country and asked if they would be willing to join my staff. I knew I had very little, if any, chance of getting the job, but I didn't want to go through life asking what might have happened if only I'd pursued it. I did some radio interviews and put my interest out there so Ohio State might give me some consideration.

On January 8, 2001, Stef gave birth to Macy, our third child. From the hospital room at Ohio State, I could look out the window and see Ohio Stadium. I thought, *Boy, is this fate?* It seemed a little crazy, but I'd grown so intoxicated by the idea of becoming head coach that I looked for positive signs anywhere I could get them. Right after that, I got a call from Andy Geiger, the athletic director at Ohio State, asking me to come over to his house to interview with him and Archie Griffin, one of Andy's assistants. They wanted me to interview on the day we planned to bring Macy home from the hospital.

I thought about calling them back and telling them I couldn't do it, but Stef jumped all over me. "Get your butt over there," she said. So I grabbed the notebook I had prepared, with printouts of game plans and practice plans, put on a coat and tie, and headed over to Andy's house in Upper Arlington. Everything went pretty well except for when I tried to address how I would share some of my pay with my assistant coaches in order to attract a better staff. I don't think Andy appreciated my ideas. "We pay our coaches fine," he said.

I went home feeling good about the interview, but never thought I would actually get the job. I knew they had interviewed some better-qualified candidates, such as Mike Bellotti, Glen Mason, and Jim Tressel. Ten days after my interview, they hired Coach Tressel. That night at a basketball game against Michigan, he made his famous promise to fans that they would be proud of his team "in the classroom, in the community and, most especially, in 310 days in Ann Arbor, Michigan."

A few days later, while everyone in town was still buzzing about that remark, Stef went in for a post-delivery checkup. She wanted to ask the doctor about a persistent cough that started in the latter months of her pregnancy. We didn't consider it significant, but I also understood that a harmless thing for someone else might be significant for someone with a history of breast cancer. Since I knew all the doctors from our work with the fund, I asked one of them to give me a call at home as soon as they ruled out anything dangerous.

The phone rang before Stef drove the short distance to our house from the hospital. Dr. William Farrar, the surgical oncologist who performed Stef's mastectomy almost three years earlier, got right to the point. "Chris, we have some tough news. The cancer has spread to her lung."

I stood there, trying to come to grips with the terrible news, praying that I could hold myself together, when the sound of the garage door told me Stef had returned home. She didn't know what the doctors had discovered. I tried to collect myself, knowing the news I had to tell her and how it would devastate her. I opened the door from the house into the garage and saw her, standing on the driver's side, reaching into the back seat to get Macy out of her baby seat. I stood there, watching Stef, mustering every ounce of inner strength I had to remain composed.

Stef came around the back of the car toward the door to the house, holding Macy in her car seat. Our eyes met. Stef stopped in her tracks and instantly *knew*. The look on my face gave it away. Neither of us spoke as the silence, even though it lasted only a few seconds, magnified the despair that gripped both of us. "This can't be happening," I finally said. "This can't be happening."

My heart broke. She realized that whatever I knew had shaken me to my core. I tried never to let Stef see me like that, but this time, the desperation nearly overwhelmed me. I struggled to bear up under the weight of our worst fears coming true.

We hugged and Stef said, "Please, don't blame Macy." That was vintage Stef. She knew that some people thought women in remission increased their odds of re-diagnosis by becoming pregnant. The doctors assured us during her pregnancy that no scientific study bore out that claim. But now, in the first minutes after learning that something had gone gravely wrong—when anybody else in the world would have focused on their own mortality and how long they might live to see their baby grow up—Stef's first thought focused on someone other than herself. "Please," she said a second time, "don't blame Macy."

We went into the house and sat down. I still hadn't told her the official word from Dr. Farrar, but my reaction already told her everything she needed to know. "I talked to the doctor, and it's gone to your lung," I said. We talked for a while, held each other, and tried to make sense of this crushing news. We found ourselves almost paralyzed by despair, trying to make sense of a future that once seemed so bright, but now held mostly fear and dread.

Eventually, the time came for me to pick up Maddie and Noah from school. I left home, but as I drove to get them, the weight of what we now faced began caving in on me. The spiritual agreement I'd made with God after Stef's first diagnosis—an agreement dictated on my own terms, not respectful of Him—had disintegrated. Almost three years earlier, when I sat up nights watching infomercials, promising God I wouldn't bother him for anything if he just helped Stef get through chemo, I'd been foolish enough to think I could bargain my way out of this nightmare. Those trivial, joking conversations I had with Jesus indicated I still felt I had some control in this situation.

Now I realized that I had *no* power to control *anything*. I'd deluded myself all along. I couldn't hide any longer from my complete and total inadequacy. I couldn't manage any of this on my own.

Emotionally devastated and spiritually beaten down, I couldn't summon the strength to drive directly to Maddie and Noah's school. Instead, I pulled behind a restaurant on Lane Avenue, got out of the car, and crawled into the back seat. I curled up into a ball and sobbed, "I can't do this. I can't go." I looked at my watch. It was late already. Maddie and Noah were waiting. I felt like a babbling fool, like a coward. Curled in the back seat in the fetal position, I screamed: "God, no more deals. I'm done."

Almost immediately, I felt a surge of strength, and a Bible verse popped into my mind: "My grace is sufficient for you, for my power is made perfect in weakness" (2 Corinthians 12:9). That encouragement from God strengthened me so I could compose myself enough to pick up Maddie and Noah, drive them home, and begin dealing with this newest challenge in our lives. This time, it wouldn't depend on my power or on my discipline and toughness as a football player.

This time, it would come from the strength God provided.

CHAPTER 14

THE MIRACLE BABY

AFTER THE RE-DIAGNOSIS IN EARLY 2001, STEF PLACED ONE OF HER first calls to her sister Sue, in Cincinnati. Sue and her husband, Bill, had been praying about where to relocate his medical practice. Bill's group worked out of Christ Hospital, where I'd had my neck fusion surgery in 1997. They had offers to go to either Columbus or Colorado, but couldn't make a case for one over the other. Then Stef called her big sister and spoke two simple but powerful words:

"It's back."

Bill and Sue's decision over where to move had kept them awake at night. They'd asked God to give them a clear direction. When Stef called with the news, they looked at each other and said, "There's our answer."

Because we made a decision as a couple to go public with Stef's battle in 1998, we had no choice now but to do the same thing as she faced breast cancer for the second time. The fund's overwhelming support from the public had, in some ways, made Stef's battle everyone's battle. It seemed only right to be out front about it, so we acknowledged in media interviews that Stef had been re-diagnosed and prepared for round two of the fight.

This time we faced a Stage IV metastatic breast cancer, which meant the disease had been detected someplace other than in the breast. We knew from our conversations with doctors three years earlier that the cancer could travel elsewhere. In all likelihood, the cancer already had moved to Stef's lung back then; it just couldn't be detected. Now we would work with a different team of doctors, ones who specialized in metastatic breast cancer. Our new oncologist would be Dr. Charles Shapiro. He explained that the cancer cells might have been in Stef's lung five to ten years before detection.

At our first meeting with Dr. Shapiro, I tried to convey my confidence in him as our newest teammate in this battle. "You're the quarterback," I said. "Move the ball." I found out later that my words, rather than encouraging him, had intimidated him. He didn't understand that by calling him our teammate, I meant to welcome him into our circle. I wanted him to know we had full confidence in him. Over the next eight years, Dr. Shapiro became a tremendous blessing in our lives, not only as a talented physician but also as a very good friend.

Stef began her second round of chemo on March 27, 2001. Our second Champions luncheon came on April 25. By then her hair had started to fall out, so she cut it short and dyed it blonde. We knew it would be a difficult day. We wanted so badly to maintain our composure and honor the recipients of the Champions award without making the event a pity party for us. Stef and I both despised pity, yet at the same time we were hurting because of the uncertainty ahead. We didn't anticipate coming away from that afternoon riding an emotional high, but the outpouring of support and the motivation from those who had beaten cancer twice provided a huge emotional lift. "Hearing those stories of others gives me strength and encourages me every day," Stef told the audience.

The second round of chemotherapy involved two drugs. Stef took Paclitaxel intravenously to kill the cancer cells. The doctors also injected her with Herceptin, a drug new to the market. It would, they hoped, build a barrier to confine the disease from spreading beyond her lungs. In combination, the two medications caused fewer side effects than Stef's initial chemo treatment in 1998. She didn't suffer nearly as much nausea this time, but she still battled chemo fog, which compromised her memory and thinking ability. She also fought a new symptom, neuropathy, or numbness, in her hands and feet.

By late November, doctors noticed sufficient shrinkage in the tumors to justify discontinuing the Paclitaxel. The numbness went away soon after that—but then a new problem surfaced.

Stef came into the family room one day and said, "Something's wrong." Alarms instantly went off in my head. Maybe other cancer husbands didn't instantly think the worst, but that's how I usually reacted. She told me she had some tightness in her abdomen. I jumped to the conclusion, "It's spread to her stomach. It's uterine cancer." While I didn't *say* that—outwardly, I tried to appear positive—inside, I went into panic mode.

Just to eliminate one possibility, Stef took a home pregnancy test. Maybe that would explain things. As I expected, the test came back negative. We'd taken precautions not to get pregnant.

Stef called and made an immediate appointment to see her OB-GYN, Dr. Mark Landon. We went in together, and he tried to calm us. "Just to be sure, let's do another pregnancy test." To our surprise—and enormous relief—the test came back positive.

We felt overjoyed, but right away I could tell we had a problem. Dr. Landon's eyes had an unmistakable look of fear and uncertainty. Where did that come from? What did that mean? He explained that because Stef was taking Herceptin, we needed to meet with her cancer doctors to discuss the ramifications of the drug on the pregnancy.

That meeting took place the next day. They explained that no baby had yet been born with the mother taking Herceptin. That left us with three choices: First, Stef could stop taking Herceptin, which might allow the cancer cells to spread and endanger her life. The Herceptin, they explained, already might have damaged the baby in her womb. Second, we could terminate the pregnancy and she could continue taking Herceptin. Third, she could stay on the drug and have the baby, not knowing whether the medication would severely impact the baby or have no effect at all.

We drove home without much conversation. It tortured us to know that whatever decision we made might cause us to lose one life, or maybe two. Because of our faith, we never would have considered abortion an option under normal circumstances. We had no doubt that God had a plan for this child's life. Now we faced a test of our beliefs. This would be a defining moment. Did we really stand for what we claimed? Did we really believe in the sanctity of human life and that life began at conception? It seemed to both of us the perfect time to apply the wisdom of Proverbs 3:5–6, which says, "Trust in the LORD with all your heart and lean not on your own understanding; in all your ways submit to him, and he will make your paths straight." We felt strongly we should trust in God's provision and step out in faith, so we agreed not to terminate the pregnancy. Stef would have our baby, and we would rely on God to keep her safe while she continued to take Herceptin.

Up to that point, there had been children born to mothers who stopped taking Herceptin when they discovered their pregnancy. There also had been monkeys born in laboratory testing whose mothers had been given massive amounts of Herceptin, far more than Stef. But she would be the first woman to have a child while continuing a Herceptin regimen.

We had an ultrasound in early May 2002. It's always amazing to see your child in the womb. We felt that same sense of wonder again, even though we'd already gone down this road three times. Besides giving us a look at the baby, the ultrasound also revealed a dangerously low level of amniotic fluid, which introduced a significant complication. The low fluid level might compromise the baby's nourishment and the development of its lungs.

The doctors began monitoring Stef's pregnancy even more closely. Did the Herceptin cause this problem? Would the baby be able to survive? Would it be born with respiratory issues that it might not be able to overcome? We didn't know the answers because no one knew the answers. No precedent existed to put our minds at ease over what might happen with this pregnancy under these circumstances.

On the first day of July, Stef saw Dr. Landon for an examination and another ultrasound to monitor the baby's development. The amniotic fluid had dipped to a dangerous level. "Go check yourself into the hospital," he said. "We're having this baby now."

They induced labor and Stef delivered Audrey one month ahead of schedule. The nurses handed her to me for just a second before they whisked her away. We had considerably more doctors in the room for this birth than for a routine birth, since Audrey was the first baby ever born with the mom taking Herceptin. They rushed Audrey away so fast, I thought, *What did we just do here?* Their reaction gave me some uneasy moments, but they brought her back to the delivery room pretty quickly and said she had checked out just fine. Stef had no problems either. After all the concern and uncertainty over the previous months, God had given us what every family hopes for—a healthy mom and a beautiful healthy baby.

The whole experience left me overwhelmingly grateful and completely amazed by the courage of Stef, doing something no mother had ever done before. Stef completely trusted God with the whole thing. I marveled at her peace. What an encouragement she offered to other women in her situation who would face the same dilemma—pregnant while taking Herceptin.

Audrey stayed in the hospital for about a month before she came home. She had no respiratory issues and was perfect in every way. Like our other three children, she had her own unique identity.

Maddie, our oldest.

Noah, our only son.

Macy, whom Stef called her angel because that pregnancy exposed the cough that led doctors to find the cancer before it could spread beyond her lung.

And now Audrey, Stef's miracle baby, the first in the world born while her mother was on Herceptin.

CHAPTER 15

MAKING THINGS RIGHT

IN ANY THRIVING CHRISTIAN MARRIAGE, THE BIRTH OF A CHILD deepens the love between a husband and a wife and bonds them together even more tightly. Our marriage grew in those same ways and, combined with the recent circumstances in our lives, left us almost euphoric after Audrey's safe arrival. We had now added two more children since Stef's first breast cancer diagnosis, which offered a powerful testimony to her courage, strength, and resilience. She absolutely would not allow *anything* to deter her from realizing our dreams.

In the previous eighteen months, she had undergone a second rigorous chemotherapy regimen and delivered two beautiful, healthy baby girls, one of whom came into the world in such a way to provide valuable research in the study of breast cancer treatment. I always knew I'd married an amazing woman. Now I realized it on a whole different level.

But despite Stef's remarkable attitude and our joy over the growth of our family, the discovery that breast cancer had spread to her lung ushered an unwelcome companion into our home.

Fear.

After Stef's initial period of remission in 1999, I pretty much convinced myself that she had healed permanently. Upon finding the cancer in the lung in 2001, we knew the cancer had reached Stage IV. I'd done enough research to know what *that* meant. In someone her age, she likely would die of metastatic breast cancer. We had fallen dangerously behind in this race. Cancer had a head start. We desperately needed advances in treatment and research to make up the distance and allow us to win.

At around age eight or nine, I had seen a TV movie called *Death Be Not Proud*. It starred Robby Benson as a kid who died from a malignant brain tumor. That really shook me up. It seemed so real to me that I went into panic mode every time my brother, Rick, got a headache. I'd run to my parents and say, "Does Rick have a brain tumor? We have to get him to the hospital. It might be something serious." I lived with that constant fear for even the slightest ache or pain felt by anyone in our family. Eventually I outgrew it, but it tormented me in a very real way for a few years.

Now I lived with that same sort of fear, but not because of something irrational prompted by a movie. This was real. It brought a nagging presence into my life because of the reality squarely in front of us. Cancer didn't frighten Stef in the same way it did me. She handled it better than I did. I never slept well on the night before she went in for tests. I'd look over at her and she'd be sleeping soundly. Her sense of peace, her faith that God would sustain her regardless of the circumstances, both inspired me and humbled me.

We lived in three-month chunks—the time between CT scans and PET scans. Those tests revealed whether her cancer had advanced and required more treatment. We rode an emotional wave when the results came back promising, but that high lasted only until I'd start fighting the urge to worry about the next test. The anxiety magnified over the final week until the test actually took place. If we received good results, then I could relax again.

Over and over, we lived that cycle, month after month, until February 2005 when the scans indicated the tumor in Stef's lung had grown enough to merit a third round of chemotherapy. The Herceptin she kept taking after delivering Audrey had worked well enough to confine the cancer to Stef's lung. At least we had that one bit of good news to hold on to.

Like a trooper, Stef fought her way through treatment and again beat back the cancer. By now, we had pretty much resigned ourselves to the tumor progressing and requiring attention every two years.

Chemo drugs have only so much impact, which makes the need for continued research so vital to the fight. Cancer cells are amazingly, maddeningly adaptive. They build up a resistance to whatever treatment targets them. The effectiveness of any regimen—whether drugs, chemo, or radiation—decreases the longer it's administered.

For that reason, it didn't surprise us two years later, in February 2007, when Stef's scans showed the cancer progressing again and in need of more attention. Dr. Shapiro recommended two oral medications yet to become available at The James but soon to arrive. Stef had no symptoms and the cancer's growth rate didn't raise immediate alarm, so we decided to wait for the oral medications. That way, Stef wouldn't have some of the side effects of intravenous chemotherapy.

While we waited for those drugs, we decided to do something the Bible calls for in times of dire health situations. James 5:14 says, "Is anyone among you sick? Let them call the elders of the church to pray over them and anoint them with oil in the name of the Lord." We believed in the power of prayer. We had never done an anointing with oil, and we felt prompted to do it as an expression of our faith. But we also knew that God's healing, His ultimate restorative power, sometimes doesn't come until we are united with Him in heaven.

Three pastors from Columbus churches came to the house with our own church elders. Together they prayed over Stefanie while anointing her with oil as they laid their hands on her.

Later that week, we went into The James for some routine testing. Before starting a treatment regimen, doctors always perform a baseline test. They can then compare all future tests with the initial results to determine the effectiveness of the chemotherapy.

Stef received a call the next day from Dr. Shapiro. She wrote an email to her friends about their conversation:

> *Dear friends:*
>   *Do you believe in the power of prayer? My answer is, yes, even more so after tonight.*
>   *This past week, Chris invited three pastors over, along with their elders, and they all prayed over me.... It was a beautiful experience.*

Prayers were precise, detailed, descriptive. "Enough, Lord. Holy Spirit, enter those cancer cells. Take this burden from them," are just a few words that echo in my head as I type. We knew I was heading into chemo again and I was having pre-chemo scans done this week, so this prayer time brought peace to the usual anxiety-filled anticipation.

Get this: My doc called tonight with the results of the tests and said the CT scan showed no growth. PET scan came back clear in every organ other than lung. Those PET scans pick up every detail out there, and we would expect changes since there had been growth in my lung in the previous two scans, but there are none. These results were excellent news and I thought would be enough, but then he added the topper. He said, "We don't need to do chemo anymore!"

We are in awe. We are so humbled. We are so thankful. We knew God COULD do it. We just didn't know if he WOULD do it, and He did. It doesn't matter if it lasts until the next scan in three months or if it lasts a couple of years. The point is, He answered our prayers!

The silly side of me is saying it's like the lyrics in that famous song. God says, "Signed, sealed, delivered, I'm yours!" I'm here to remind you, He's yours too.

Thank you for all your thoughts and prayers. I am blessed by you all.

> *In Him,*
> *Stef*

When the God of the universe offers a miracle in response to your heartfelt prayers, it thrills you and humbles you at the same time. Obviously, we hoped God's provision would become permanent. But Stef's email emphasized that the duration of the miracle had far less significance to us than the magnitude of it being granted. So when she suffered an alarming coughing fit later that summer, we wondered how long this latest miracle would last.

We had decided to rent an RV for our vacation, and I joked that I dreaded only one thing about that trip: emptying the toilet. So I looked for any way to *avoid* having that duty fall to me.

On this particular day, we had set out for Grand Beach on the shores of Lake Michigan to meet my brother Rick and his wife,

Michelle, at a cabin they had rented. Rick's job as general manager of the Minnesota Vikings kept our families from getting together very often, so we expected this to be a special time.

Stef made sure to stock the RV's kitchen with food and snacks, and our daughters—Madison, thirteen; Macy, six; and Audrey, five —packed their bicycles and plenty of swimsuits for the week ahead. The girls and I had agreed that their brother, Noah, should handle toilet detail. Most eleven-year-old boys would object, and no doubt Noah would have too; but he didn't get a vote, since the week before our vacation he was attending a church camp in southern Indiana.

We began our trip by driving out of Columbus, Ohio, on I–70, then headed south from Indianapolis to pick up Noah. Predictably, he didn't take his election to toilet detail without a fight, so that made for some good-natured teasing as we traveled north through Indiana and toward the lake.

After about an hour, the kids started to settle in the back of the RV. I expected a quiet drive the rest of the way to Rick's cabin.

But right about then, Stef started to cough and suffer serious chest pains.

Despite my years in the NFL, playing with all sorts of injuries and watching other players do the same, I knew nobody tougher than my wife. I had watched her handle the horrible side effects of chemotherapy and get stuck by more needles than I could count. Yet she never complained once or asked, "Why me?"

For that reason, I'd learned that on the rare occasions when she acknowledged pain or discomfort, I had to take it seriously. And now she looked to be in significant distress, with us two hundred miles from home and who knows how far from the nearest hospital—and with our four children suddenly wide awake and wondering what had gone wrong with their mom.

Both Stef and I always tried to shield our kids from worrying about her condition. We never lied to them about her illness, but they didn't need to know a lot of details about her cancer and her treatment. We didn't want them worrying every day about whether she'd be okay.

This time, though, Stef and I had no other room to step into and talk. We couldn't send the kids upstairs to bed. We couldn't call a sitter and then rush to the hospital. But we had to do something and we had to do it *now*.

A few months earlier, Stef had suffered the same symptoms at Noah's spring talent show at school. I'd watched Noah sing "Amazing Grace" and then left early with our two youngest girls to put them to bed. Stef stayed behind to watch the rest of the program and bring Noah home. She started having problems after I left.

Stef's sister, Sue, and her physician husband, Bill, were at the talent show that night, watching Noah sing. When they brought Stef home, I immediately knew something wasn't right. Bill took me aside and told me that the problem could be a pulmonary embolism and that I should take Stef to the hospital. A pulmonary embolism is a blockage in the main artery to the lung. Once Bill told me it could be fatal, I didn't need to hear any more. I rushed Stef to the emergency room, where doctors put her through a series of tests. Sometime later they called it a false alarm. They couldn't explain what it was or why it happened.

Now as we traveled in the RV, I hoped this latest episode would turn out to be another false alarm. Maybe—but since we didn't know for sure, Stef dialed her doctor.

"Get to an emergency room right away," Dr. Shapiro ordered.

I exited I–65 as quickly as possible and pulled into a truck stop. I ran inside and asked the woman at the counter for directions to the nearest hospital.

"It's right up the road," she said, "about four miles."

I found it within ten minutes—Witham Memorial Hospital in Lebanon, Indiana. It looked like a ghost town when we pulled into the parking lot. I told the kids to just sit tight for a while until I got Stef inside to get her checked out.

Fortunately, no one waited ahead of us in line, so they immediately took her in for an examination. For the next two hours, I alternated between remaining inside with Stef while she took tests and running back outside to the RV to check on the kids. None of them had panicked, because they'd grown accustomed to their mom requiring medical attention. She also made frequent trips to the doctor for checkups, so while this was out of the ordinary, it didn't scare them like it might have other kids with moms who rarely, if ever, get sick. In order not to alarm them, I focused on acting as calm as possible.

Inside, I was a basket case.

Would Stef be okay? If this turned out to be something serious, how would we get her back to Columbus? Had the doctors back home missed something last spring when Stef had this problem before? And if so, had it grown worse?

One minute we'd been driving on the highway, a few hours away from a lake cabin and a fun week of vacation for our family with my brother and his family. And now I was standing in the kitchen of an RV, opening a can of SpaghettiOs for my kids, who were riding their bicycles in the hospital parking lot of an unfamiliar little town. Meanwhile, my wife was inside, possibly having a serious issue with her heart or lungs.

I felt as helpless as I ever had at any time in my life.

I'd known that same frustration many times since Stef's diagnosis. No matter how many times I experienced it, I never grew accustomed to it and it never became any easier to handle. Now, like countless times before, I wanted answers.

I wanted them for Stef.

I wanted them for me.

I wanted them for our kids.

I wanted to know why Stef was hurting.

I wanted to know how to make it stop hurting.

I wanted her to get better.

I wanted this nightmare—this lousy Saturday night and this whole cancer ordeal—to be over.

But like most of the time, on this night we got no answers at all.

The emergency room doctors from Witham Memorial told us they just couldn't explain what caused Stef's chest pains or her coughing fit. They had no more answers for us than our own doctors did. They couldn't explain why those symptoms came out of nowhere or why they had begun to diminish.

"Everything checks out okay," they said. "We don't see anything out of the ordinary."

It was a huge relief. And yet, it was no relief at all.

Stef felt wiped out from the ordeal, but she knew how much the kids had looked forward to this vacation. Always the soldier, she insisted we get back on schedule. So off we drove into the night, headed toward Lake Michigan.

The following year, tests showed that she needed to have chemo again. And once again, she faced the news head-on.

By then, The James had the two oral cancer drugs we had waited for at the time of her 2007 diagnosis. Stef began taking Ticurb and Xaloda in November 2008. Neither drug had many side effects. People who saw her never knew the severity of Stef's condition. The drugs worked marvelously, and she looked and felt fine.

Life was good ... except for some sobering news we received earlier that year on another front.

In March 2008, while on vacation in the Florida Keys on spring break, my dad called to tell me he had colon cancer. He didn't want to tell me, but his fiancée made him place the call. He downplayed it. "I'll be fine. It's nothing. Don't worry."

He and my mom had divorced in 1994, during my next-to-last year with the Lions. There are two sides to every story, but I still blamed my dad for the divorce. Children automatically blame someone, and I blamed him, probably because I had placed him on an unfair pedestal. The divorce made me bitter and, for a while, really crushed my perception of him. Not that I didn't love him, but I had a very empty feeling about the whole situation. We kind of drifted apart, but I never stopped talking to him; I just couldn't bring myself to cut him off. He was one of my better friends in the world. At one time, we had had an extremely strong relationship. Then it cooled and became lukewarm, at best, until we mended things. He lived in Florida during that time, so I didn't see him much. We finally had some heart-to-heart talks and worked through some things, but it took a while to rekindle our relationship.

I knew I had to try, because God made that clear in the fifth of the Ten Commandments: "Honor your father and mother ..." I took that command very seriously even though it hurt to see my mom and dad's marriage end.

Doctors found the colon cancer when my father was still coaching. He'd worked the Ohio State coaching clinic for years, even after he retired from Massillon. One year, while working the clinic, he ran into a high school coach from Florida who asked him to come down to be his assistant. My dad took the job despite being in his late sixties. He called me one day and said, "I'm driving to Florida. I have a coaching job."

After they found his colon cancer, he returned to Ohio and spent most of his time at Mercy Hospital in Canton, formerly Timken Mercy Hospital, where I was born. He had a cabin at Atwood Lake, near Canton, where he normally spent his summers. It's how he wound up back in Ohio for treatment. I spent a lot of days that summer driving up from Columbus to see him during chemo.

Eventually, I had my dad moved to The James. I wanted to make sure he would get the best care possible, and it made it easier to see him every day. Those days helped our relationship. We talked a lot. We talked about football. We talked about life. We talked about faith. We talked about things we wished we hadn't let get away. Our talks didn't make either of us sad. We had some really good conversations.

By spending all that time with him, it felt as though we reached a peace with where we ended up as father and son. I always admired him, not just as my dad, but as a man. I admired his work ethic. I also admired my mother's. It would be unfair for me not to include her. They both showed me what it meant to sacrifice for your children.

Right about the time I grew comfortable again being around my dad, without any unspoken tension between us, he started to struggle with an assortment of issues. He had cardiovascular issues, he began bleeding internally, and then his lungs filled with fluid. Things kept compounding until doctors had to put him on a ventilator so he could breathe. The ventilator kept him from talking. He tried to talk, but I struggled to make out what he said. For months, I sat with him in the

Intensive Care Unit, with me talking about the old times to help him get through the day.

When Rick and I were kids, my dad had two paddles he used on us—the Masher and the Stinger. Dad made the Stinger out of a table in our basement that Rick and I ruined. One day we got bored, so we pounded a bunch of nails into our dad's work table. That really made him angry. The nails protruded through the top, so he hacksawed off the ends of the nails as close to the surface as he could. He couldn't get the entire nail, so when he swatted us with the Stinger, we felt every one of those nails we'd pounded in. Eventually, we graduated to the Masher, a smaller paddle that gathered more speed as he swung it. He wrapped a bunch of athletic tape around it and wrote our names on it.

As a kid, I loved matches. One time, my dad caught me playing with them and told me, "Go get the Masher." I bent over, touched my toes, and braced for impact. He cracked me hard across the rear end. I knew he admired toughness in his players, so I popped right up and looked him in the eye, showing him that the Masher hadn't hurt me at all. You know what he did? He told me to bend my butt over again. He wound up and cracked me even harder. That didn't hurt much either, but I pretended that it did. I cried, just so he wouldn't go for round three.

Now, as he lay there in the hospital bed, I asked if he remembered the time he cracked me with the Masher and I didn't flinch. He nodded. I reminded him that he told me to bend over again. He nodded. Then I asked if he remembered me crying after the second one. He nodded. "Well," I said, "you should know something. I faked it." He laughed so hard the tracheotomy tube in his throat popped out. The alarms went off, and nurses came running in to save him.

My dad loved to dance, so we would watch *Dancing with the Stars, So You Think You Can Dance*, and lots of sports. One night in the ICU, one dancer made an incredible leap. "Dad," I said, "wouldn't that guy have made a great cornerback?" He started laughing and nodding his head.

Those lighter moments tempered the difficulty he had with the ventilator. He hated that thing. He talked about wanting to pull the plug and die. That's what he told me, but he'd tell his fiancée something different. I wanted him to make that decision, because he still had all his mental faculties. One time he mouthed the words, "I can't take this anymore." I asked if he wanted the ventilator turned off. He said, "No." Then he said, "Yeah." And then, "No." He would often say, "I have to get out of here and get back to Florida and coaching." But after he went in for chemo in March, he never came back out.

He had some very tough days toward the end. I got a call late in the summer to rush up to Canton, to the rehab facility where he spent his last months. They told me he wouldn't make it through the night. A priest even came to give him last rites. But my dad pulled through and lived a couple more months. That happened several times. It seemed that every time they told us he wouldn't live much longer, he improved and got better.

A children's book, *Love You Forever*, reminded me of how things had come full circle with my dad and me. The book begins with the birth of a son. His mother is rocking him to sleep, saying she'll love him forever, that as long as she lives, "My baby you'll be." At the end of the book, the boy, now a man, is holding his elderly mother and saying that he'll love her forever, and as long as he lives, "My Mommy you'll be."* I had a vision of that book when I carried my dad to the bathroom and assisted him with some of the things he could no longer do for himself.

Dad died on October 13, 2008. When I got the call, I had this overwhelming sense of relief. People with a strong faith in Christ —people who have an eternal perspective, who know that our home here is just a temporary dwelling place—feel relief when an ailing loved one dies. Dying spared my dad the continued misery of being stuck to a tube in a bed for twenty-four hours a day. I took comfort in knowing he was in paradise and no longer in pain. I said a prayer of thanksgiving. While that might sound unfeeling to some, I genuinely felt thankful. I didn't want my dad to suffer anymore. He fought to the end. He didn't receive his healing in this life. Sometimes, that doesn't come until God calls us home.

---

*Robert Munsch, *Love You Forever* (Buffalo, NY: Firefly, 1986).

My dad lived for seventy-one years and was the only person ever to coach Timken to an unbeaten season. That 8–0–1 record in 1974 also marked the last time Timken had back-to-back winning seasons. I joked at his funeral, "I'm sure he's got eleven apostles lined up right now and one ready to come off the bench." Because my dad knew Jesus as his personal Savior, I didn't cry at his memorial service. As tough and proud as he was, he wasn't too tough or too proud to recognize his sin and acknowledge his need to have Christ save him. Through faith, my dad received God's forgiveness by choosing to accept Christ. That's why he'll live forever in heaven. I couldn't make that choice for him, and he couldn't make it for me. Every person in the world has to make that decision at some time, either to accept Christ and receive eternal life with God or reject him and bear the consequences.

I felt sad to lose my dad, but I knew I would see him again someday in heaven. I focused on being glad for his life, for the time he had, and for the time I had with him. Because his illness had lasted so long, I had moved past saying, "Why, Lord?" Instead, I focused on, "Thank You for this day."

And, "If it's Your will, thank You for tomorrow."

CHAPTER 16

I Can't Spell "Tennis"

We developed a saying in our house over the years: "Today is a good day. Tomorrow looks good. After that, we don't know." It was a brutally honest way of looking at our life and the constant unpredictability of the cancer cells in Stef's body having the potential to pounce without warning.

A lot of people strive to live for the moment. For us, it was a way of life we grew into because we understood that nothing in this life was promised to us. For that reason, we cherished any family time we could get. That's why we were so excited about sailing on the Buckeye Cruise for Cancer in February 2009.

The idea for the cruise came from Lisa Cisco, who approached Stef to fill a Royal Caribbean cruise ship with two thousand Ohio State fans to raise money for cancer research. We helped recruit about twenty former Ohio State athletes—most of them football players —for a four-day, three-night cruise. The first event in 2008 went over so well that more than half the people on board were ready to sign up for a second cruise before the inaugural cruise even ended.

Of all the fundraising events Stef and I attended since her first diagnosis in July 1998, the second Buckeye Cruise would be the first one attended by our entire family and by Stef's mother and my mother. So, with an attitude of excitement and anticipation, the eight of us boarded a flight February 10 and flew from Columbus to Tampa, where the cruise would depart two days later.

Stef had been fighting a cough for months, but otherwise she felt pretty good. We had a scare in August, six months earlier, when Dr.

142

Shapiro detected an increase in the size of the tumor in her lung. Stef started chemo again, for the fourth time, taking Doxyl intravenously along with Herceptin. When Stef tried Doxyl in her initial round of chemo in 1998, Herceptin hadn't yet been developed.

Dr. Shapiro, always on top of the latest developments, told us that Doxyl could be packaged in a new way and then combined with Herceptin to fight the cancer cells more effectively. As a bonus, the drugs taken together wouldn't cause Stef to lose any of her hair. So, despite the chemo, no one outside the family suspected anything. She appeared perfectly healthy.

Every previous chemo regimen lasted for six months, but this time, Dr. Shapiro called a halt to things in January, after four months. Some parts of the tumor had decreased in size and others hadn't responded at all. The mixed results caused him no concern; nor did he give us any false hope that everything would turn out fine. That's one of many reasons we liked him so much. He always shot straight with us, which we appreciated.

Dr. Shapiro answered most of our questions, but he couldn't explain Stefanie's cough. "Persistent" doesn't begin to convey its severity. She coughed constantly and went through as many as forty cough drops every day. I hoped the warmer weather in Tampa and on the cruise might cure her cough. Very quickly, though, I developed much bigger concerns. Stef's energy on board ship didn't begin to approach her normal level. As a cancer husband, you get a sense for when a seemingly innocuous thing becomes anything but. I felt in my gut that something must be wrong, but as we sailed that first night from Tampa to Key West, I buried my concern. I didn't want to ruin this trip, which all of us were really looking forward to, by being an alarmist. I tried to convince myself I had invented something that didn't exist. But deep down, I suspected trouble.

Typically in these situations, Stef would channel her old cheerleader days at Jackson High School and become the ringleader for everything. In her years as a public figure in the fight against breast cancer, giving hundreds of speeches at scores of fundraising events, Stef always rose to the occasion. No matter how she felt, she had mastered the art of hiding the toll cancer took on her. She never, *ever* let on if she felt sick. No one else in our group picked up on her condition—not her mom, not my mom, and not the kids—but she couldn't hide it from me. I'd known this woman since she'd turned fifteen. Ever since her first diagnosis, I trained myself to stay on high alert for every symptom and side effect. She could fool everyone else, but she'd long since lost the ability to fool me.

The next morning, after we arrived in Key West for a quick stop on our way to Playa del Carmen in Mexico, I became even more convinced of my suspicions while listening to Stef do a radio interview. She talked about the fund, the medical advancements it helped finance at The James, and how the previous eleven years had produced a net positive for our family—given all the benefits of our experiences when stacked against the negatives of the disease. She did a great job, but she didn't fool me at all. I knew *something* was wrong because she struggled throughout the interview just to get her words out. She always sounded sharp and polished whenever she did an interview, so her hesitation convinced me that something wasn't right.

Later that weekend, I confided my fears to a friend on board as our family got ready to spend the day at the beach in Mexico.

"Stef sure looks great," he said to me.

"Remember what I told you about her," I replied.

"What was that?" he said.

"She's a great faker. Something isn't right. I just know it."

Whatever had gone wrong, I couldn't do anything about it over the next two days, floating on a cruise ship in the Gulf of Mexico. But I resolved that once we returned to Columbus, we'd meet with Dr. Shapiro and get to the bottom of this.

Stef maintained a great front the rest of the weekend, but she began heading downhill fast as we flew home on Monday. Her coughing increased, and she grew extremely dizzy and exhausted. I hoped her condition came from riding a ship on intermittently rough seas, trying to press through her fatigue and stay up late to play her role as hostess. I wanted to believe that so badly that I called a friend after we got back to town and asked him about his battle with vertigo a few months before. I hoped to find a plausible explanation for Stef's symptoms. I didn't want to face what I feared the most.

The answer came swiftly the next morning, when Stefanie called my cell phone shortly after leaving the house to take the kids to school. "I'm having trouble driving," she said. "I'm really dizzy."

I tried to encourage her. I blamed it on the side effects of the cruise and asked if she could make it back to our house safely. She assured me she could, so I left an appointment downtown and hurried home to meet her. When I arrived, her car was already in the garage. I ran in the house and bounded up the stairs two at a time. I burst into our room and saw her sitting on the bed, looking at her cell phone, crying.

She looked up at me and said, "I can't spell 'tennis.'"

I walked over and looked at the screen as she tried to send a text. In place of "tennis" I saw "T3NNNNNSSSSSS."

"Call the doctor," I said.

From the moment of Stefanie's initial diagnosis twelve years earlier, she had one overriding fear, and it wasn't dying. She never feared dying, and I came to let go of that fear too. Both of us had an eternal perspective on life. We saw this life as an eyeblink compared to eternity, and we knew that if death separated us, we would be together again in heaven. We depended on that promise of Christ from the cross, available to all who believe in him. Stefanie and I had claimed that promise as our own years before, and our kids had claimed it too.

Obviously, Stef didn't want to die, nor did she treat her health in a cavalier way. She fought to *live*, not just to survive. But after her first diagnosis and once we grasped how many people we could impact and inspire with her battle—once we understood the platform cancer gave us to raise money for research, and, most importantly, understood the privilege cancer gave us to expose our shared faith in Christ and how that faith sustained us—death didn't loom as a primary fear for either of us.

From the beginning, Stef's biggest fear centered on the disease eventually spreading to her brain. She had lived that nightmare once already with her father, Dr. Richard Belcher, who died of brain cancer in 1987 two years after suffering a seizure in his living room in

Canton. So periodically throughout her battle, over four separate chemotherapy regimens, Stef insisted on a CAT scan of her brain to make
sure the disease hadn't spread there. The results always had come back
negative. Now, as we walked through the doors of The James, we had
much greater cause for concern. Her dizzy spells had grown so severe
I had to steady her so she wouldn't fall. This time, a brain scan had
merit beyond simply soothing Stefanie's long-held fears about suffering the same fate as her father. This time, we needed the brain scan
to alleviate our worst fears that the disease we had fought for so long
might be winning.

More than anything else over the previous twelve years, I came
to dread waiting for the telephone to ring, bringing test results. I'm
ashamed to admit that, because God tells us not to worry. One of my
favorite Scriptures, Philippians 4:6–7, says, "Do not be anxious about
anything, but in every situation, by prayer and petition, with thanksgiving, present your requests to God. And the peace of God, which
transcends all understanding, will guard your hearts and your minds
in Christ Jesus." I knew in my heart that I shouldn't worry, but I also
fought the human side. My concern for my wife and family overshad-
owed what I "should" do. I hated that helpless feeling when my day
revolved around, "Why isn't the phone ringing? Is the call late? Does
that mean something is wrong? Is the doctor just not caught up? Why
haven't they called yet?"

Then, when it would finally ring, my heart always jumped.

"Why are they calling so early? Did they find something? Do they
need to tell us right away?" Those emotions consistently ran through
my mind. I got so upset with myself because I felt weak and helpless,
at the mercy of a phone call, whether it brought good news or bad
news. For twelve years, I agonized over the phone call.

And now, several hours after the brain scan, I sat at home, waiting
again for the phone to ring.

When it did, and when Dr. Shapiro relayed the news to me, I felt
strangely like a man watching a movie of someone else's life, a movie
with an ending I already knew.

"Chris," he said, "the cancer has spread to Stefanie's brain."

He told me to get to the pharmacy and pick up a prescription for a drug called Decadron, which would reduce the swelling on Stef's brain. He told me we would start radiation immediately, hoping to shrink the cancer cells in her brain.

I drove to the pharmacy and waited for them to fill Dr. Shapiro's order. My cell phone rang. A friend called, just to chat.

"I can't talk right now," I said. "My life's just been turned upside down."

CHAPTER 17

YOU CAN DO IT

STEFANIE'S FIRST SIX-MONTH ROUND OF CHEMOTHERAPY, FROM August 1998 to January 1999, inflicted some brutal side effects. Her hair fell out; she puked more in single days than she had her entire life; nothing tasted good; she had no energy; and her brain fell victim to "chemo fog," where she just couldn't focus, remember much, or recall even the simplest words or phrases.

But chemo, even when new and at its most debilitating, went smoothly compared to the two weeks of radiation on her brain after doctors detected cancer there in March 2009.

Stef didn't respond well to Decadron, which doctors prescribed to reduce the swelling in her brain. It made her listless and loopy, and neither the Decadron nor the radiation did anything to reduce the dizziness that left the world spinning around her every minute of every day.

That forced us to alter the division of labor that had ruled in our marriage since Maddie's birth in 1994. Ever since then, I made the money and Stef ran the house. She paid the bills, did the shopping, cooked the meals, and organized the kids' activities. Of course, I helped with what I could after I stopped playing in the NFL, but she ran the show and thrived at handling all the demands of our busy household.

I had to assume the full-time parent role once radiation began, with lots of help from family and friends. I managed as best I could by drawing on my background as a football player. I put up charts listing each day of the week and what each child had going on. At times, the grease board in our kitchen looked more like a football game plan than our weekly schedule, but we made it work and weathered those difficult days.

Our financial adviser helped me set up a budget so I could pay the bills. Stef's way had worked for her. But now that the responsibility fell to me, I had to understand why we did things, and that involved some changes. All the while, I hoped the radiation would work, that it would kill the cancer in her brain and we could soon get back to normal.

But for now, this was our new normal.

I despised going to The James for Stef's radiation treatments. Nothing against The James, but my stomach just wretched every time we walked in there. The treatments lasted only ten or fifteen minutes each, but it felt like torture, waiting for them to end. I just couldn't stand that feeling of helplessness. I couldn't do *anything*. That had bothered me from the first minute of her battle against breast cancer, and now it bothered me even more.

Always before, whenever I had a problem in life, I took the initiative to solve it. If I couldn't fix it immediately, I out-studied it, outworked it, out-lifted it, outran it, whatever. But I had no control over this opponent. By myself, I could do nothing to defeat it. I had to rely completely on God, doctors, and medicine. I hated that feeling. I felt like a newborn baby, waiting to be fed.

After Stef completed radiation and passed her physical with Dr. Shapiro a few weeks later, we wanted to celebrate as a family. We planned a nice meal at home, with all the kids. We had the attitude, "Mom is finished with her treatments and will be getting better." After we prayed, but before we started eating, Stef excused herself to use the bathroom. She got up from the table and started to walk down the hallway.

But then she fell.

I rushed to her and she said, "My foot feels funny."

I tended to panic anytime she had a cough, a sniffle—anything. The cancer's advance to her brain put my radar on even higher alert, so her falling just as we sat down to celebrate felt like a punch to the temple. I tried not to show any visible concern because Maddie, Noah, Macy, and Audrey were sitting right there at the table, watching us. I didn't want to worry them, so I told them to go ahead with dinner. I carried Stef upstairs and called Dr. Shapiro.

He told me to test the strength of her foot by having her push up against my pressure. She had absolutely no strength at all, so I called him back with that information.

"Get to the emergency room right away," he said.

That really upset Stef. It made her angry—not at Dr. Shapiro or me, but at the situation. I tried to put up a good front. "Don't worry, we'll get it taken care of and everything will be fine." But inside, it broke my heart. *Why? Why now?*

Stef's sister Sue came over to watch the kids so we could go to the ER. Stef went through all the tests, and we waited while she rested in a recovery room.

About midnight, Dr. Shapiro called with the results. As always, he gave it to us straight: "There is cancer on Stefanie's spine and in her spinal fluid."

Now we knew. The radiation hadn't worked. The cancer cells were winning. They had survived the treatment aimed at killing them and had spread. We always knew this diagnosis might come, but we had held out hope of avoiding it. After countless tests, conventional treatments, clinical trials, untold hours waiting in agony for results, and innumerable prayers, we now faced the unrelenting reality we'd resisted with everything we had.

Stef would die of breast cancer.

In her typical soldier-on mentality, Stef calmly asked about our treatment options. We didn't decide anything at that point. We needed time to absorb what had happened. Besides, we would have to meet with a different oncologist now that the cancer had moved to Stef's spine. We couldn't make any determination right away.

She rested as night turned into early the next day. I sat and watched TV, praying whenever she dozed off. The hours passed. What do you say? What do you do after getting news like that?

Before I left to go home, Stef reached out and touched my hand as I sat beside her bed. She looked at me with some sadness and said, "You've proven to me that you can do it."

I knew exactly what she meant. She had seen me run the house while she went through radiation. That alleviated her fear that I couldn't manage things without her. That gave her real peace, and it also calmed me. I knew that concern ranked as one of her biggest fears about dying: "Man, this dude, how is he going to do it?" I relied on her so much, but in that month's time, I proved to her I could manage things.

I drove home from the hospital around 4:30 a.m. I thanked Sue for staying with the kids but didn't give her too many details about the bad news. I had something more pressing that I had to do, so I made my way upstairs.

I went into each child's bedroom and stood over each one, praying for God's mercy, for peace, strength, resilience—any warrior term I could come up with. I pleaded with God to give them the courage to handle the circumstances headed our way.

Then I tried to go into our room. I tried, but I couldn't get past the door. It made me mad at myself that I couldn't summon the strength to go in, but the reality of the previous few hours hit me hard in that moment. I felt a need to brace myself, to gather my thoughts before I went in there. I prayed for God to give me strength. Eventually, I walked in, more focused, believing that I had a plan.

I sat in Stef's favorite chair for a few minutes, and then I went into her closet and ran my hand over all her clothes. I walked over to her sink and felt compelled to brush my teeth with her toothbrush and toothpaste. Then I laid down on her side of the bed and went to sleep.

Right before I woke up that morning, I had a vision flashing in my mind. I saw a very vivid image of a rolling billboard, the kind where the message scrolls across the screen, like in Times Square. I remember exactly the color of the letters: not red, but more an orange-yellow. The message said: "No matter what, Chris, everything is going to be OK. Trust me."

I woke up and knew I had experienced one of those cherished

moments in a believer's life when you feel as though God is communicating a message directly to you. It enabled me to wake up and deal with the reality at hand with a clear mind and a sharp focus.

From that point forward, I had a peace like the Bible describes: "The peace of God, which transcends all understanding" (Philippians 4:7). I call it a tolerable peace. Along with that peace came the ability to not let the highs get too high or the lows get too low. I didn't want to get emotionally leveled again. I didn't want to get sucker-punched or devastated again. God gave me a gift—a gift of peace. It was not the gift I wanted. But it was exactly the gift I needed.

CHAPTER 18

No Doom and Gloom

RETURNING TO THE HOSPITAL THE NEXT MORNING, I BRACED FOR what I considered one of the most difficult conversations I would ever have with Stefanie. I knew the test results from the night before. All those years as a cancer husband had made me way too informed to have false hope for the future. I understood the dire reality of her diagnosis. I had no time to waste, because I didn't know how long the cancer in her brain would allow her to think clearly. And for this discussion, I desperately needed Stef sharp and focused.

But before we could talk, Dr. Michael Cavaliere, a neuro-oncologist specializing in cancer of the brain and spine, met with us to discuss Stef's treatment options. While we still were dealing with breast cancer, it now had migrated to the two most lethal areas of her body—her brain and spine. We had some radical options. Because of the severity of her cancer, Stef needed a port placed in her head so they could drip chemo directly into her brain. I asked, "What are the chances of this working?"

He looked at both of us and said, "Modest, at best."

Given that sobering assessment, I wish I could have waited to talk to Stef about the subject gnawing at me. Unfortunately, I couldn't delay any longer. I didn't know how communicative she would be or for how long she would be able to communicate. We had to talk about planning her funeral. It mattered to me more than anything that *she* make those decisions. She'd fought too hard, too long, and too courageously to leave any of her wishes unfulfilled at the finish line.

We had addressed the subject generally at various times since her first diagnosis in 1998. But this time, I needed Stef to speak as specifically as possible so I could do exactly what she wanted. I could think of no easy way to ask her. Finally I just said, as sensitively as I could, "How do you want your funeral? How do you want it done?"

Talking about it made her a little emotional, but she gave very clear instructions. I could tell she had given it a lot of thought. She emphasized a familiar phrase she had spoken often throughout her battle, one that she would repeat many more times in the coming months. "I don't want any doom and gloom," she said.

I asked if she wanted me to say a few words about her when the time came.

"You can speak," she said, "but don't talk about me. Instead, make sure you thank everyone for what they've done for us."

With that conversation out of the way, I felt a huge burden lifted.

Now I faced another difficult discussion — one with Maddie and Noah. Stef and I always had been open with them about her medical condition, explaining the situation on a level we felt they could understand. We'd long since progressed from the "Mommy-has-a-boo-boo-on-her-boobie" stage, which worked back in 1998 when Maddie was four and Noah was two. Now I had to bring them fully in on the dire situation ahead of us.

Just like my earlier conversation with Stef, I saw no easy or painless way to do this. But Maddie, nearing the end of her freshman year of high school, and Noah, only a seventh grader, had to know the truth before they heard about it from whispers in the community.

I took both of them into a room at home and said, "Mom has some issues. I don't know how these issues are going to turn out. They could turn out well or they could turn out really bad. In the meantime, I'm asking you to help me. I know this is not fair, but this is what I need from you." I told them Stef would have chemo again and work with a physical therapist. I asked them to help with the two younger girls. Both of them responded, "I understand."

Macy was eight and Audrey was six at the time. They didn't need to know anything beyond, "Mom is sick and is trying to get better."

I noticed an immediate change in Noah. He began doing new

things. He gave his little sisters their baths or he read to them. That marked quite a change. Before, like any twelve-year-old boy, he sometimes fought the urge to slam their heads together.

Maddie has such a servant's heart. She tried to do too much too soon and put enormous pressure on herself. She felt a responsibility to take the place of her mom so she could take some of the burden off me. Sue, Stef's sister, told me one night after I came home from the hospital that Maddie had gotten very emotional that evening. I took her outside to speak with her, but first I hugged her for a long time. She started to cry. "Maddie," I said, "here's the plan: I just need you to be Maddie. I need your help, but your heart will tell you when to help. You don't have to do everything. Just let your heart tell you." It was a good talk. I could sense a great deal of relief come over her.

Telling my two oldest children what we faced with Stef bonded us together even more tightly. Their reaction didn't surprise me, because the circumstances of our life over the years had trained them for this moment. Having grown up in the cancer world, they had watched Stef and me attend many funerals of people we'd met through friendships forged around the disease and its treatment. They always knew and understood what could happen. Never before, though, had I spoken to Maddie and Noah and left the outcome open regarding their own mom. This time, when I told them, "She might get better; she might get worse," they understood what that meant.

The public gained its first hint that something had gone seriously wrong in mid-April, when Stef couldn't join me to host the Stefanie's Champions luncheon at the Columbus Convention Center. It tore Stef up to miss that event—the fundraiser she had designed to thank caregivers for supporting the cancer patients in their life. She often remarked to Sue, "I've got to get better for Champions." But as the days went by, Stef realized she would have to miss it. She struggled emotionally to accept that decision, because ever since the first Champions in 2000, she looked forward to that event more than to any other on her calendar. It held a special place in her heart. It always inspired her so much to be around other survivors. Now she knew she couldn't be there to celebrate Champions' tenth anniversary.

We asked a friend, Andrea Cambern, of WBNS-TV in Columbus, to stand in for Stef at the luncheon. Andrea did a great job, but it felt surreal to me, standing up there without my wife. Getting through that program, and knowing how much it devastated Stef to stay home, took all of the inner strength I could summon. I kept telling myself not to break down. I absolutely did not want that to happen, because it would have sent the wrong message. Neither Stef nor I wanted to make the Champions luncheon about her or about us. That would have dishonored the purpose of the event, which is to help people feel they don't fight alone and to make them understand that cancer doesn't strike just the patient, it hits everyone in the family. Stef didn't want much said about her and certainly wanted nothing mentioned about the gravity of her latest diagnosis.

I prayed so much, and so hard, about that day. When the time finally came to take the stage, I felt a strength given to me by God. Only His power allowed me to get through the program without my voice breaking. I started by saying, "As you can see, I'm on my own this year." I mentioned that Stef faced some new health challenges, but didn't go into detail. Otherwise, it was business as usual.

We honored the six special caregivers, like always, and honored the survivors in attendance by having them stand for a round of applause. It looked, sounded, and felt like any other Champions luncheon despite being completely unlike any of the previous nine. This one didn't include Stefanie. In 2001, 2005, and 2007 she hosted the event while undergoing chemotherapy, inspiring everyone with her courage. This time, she inspired us by issuing a strict set of marching orders: "No doom and gloom." And when it ended, I came away thinking that we had pulled it off better than we had thought possible.

Stef's sister Sandy had arrived in town two days before the Champions luncheon. Despite all the millions of dollars spent on cancer research, no medication could have done for Stef what Sandy's arrival accomplished. Of the four Belcher girls, Sue was the oldest, Cindy came next, then Stef, and finally Sandy. As the baby sister, Sandy had a special relationship with Stef.

Sandy just dropped her life in Fort Lauderdale, took a leave from her job, and for three months fit right into our family. We could not have made it through the summer without Sandy and Sue and all the friends who pitched in to take up the slack.

Sue and her husband, Bill, moved to Columbus in 2001 when Stef's cancer returned the first time. In all that time, they had been rocks for us to lean on. Sue stepped up big-time then and always willingly did whatever we needed when Stef struggled with a setback. This time, after things went south following the cruise to Mexico, Sue essentially set her life aside to be with Stef and our kids every day. As the big sister, Sue had a protective side and a perceptive side. She understood that Stef's biggest fear had finally come true.

Typical of my wife's selfless nature, her biggest fear had nothing to do with what might happen to *her*. It had everything to do with her concern for someone else. Stef always feared the cancer would spread to her brain. She didn't fear that because she watched her father die from a brain tumor, but because she hoped to avoid subjecting her mom to that ordeal again. Stef had hoped to avoid doing what she finally had to do at The James two months earlier, when Sue stood by the bed in support as Stef picked up the phone and dialed her mom. "I'm so sorry," Stef said. "I'm so sorry to have to put you through this again." She began sobbing uncontrollably. The tears came flooding out of a reservoir of dread and worry that started with her own diagnosis in 1998.

Despite the spread of her cancer to her brain and spine, Stef was determined to participate in the Susan G. Koman Race for the Cure in downtown Columbus in May. She had made that event an annual tradition ever since her original diagnosis, running in it for the first time in 1999, just five months after completing her initial round of chemo. I pushed Noah and Maddie in the stroller that day while Stef completed the 5K run. Watching her cross the finish line inspired me more than anything I had ever seen.

Stef knew how much her battle meant to other people in the community. She realized the role she played in inspiring others by not just surviving, but thriving. Not participating, despite her limited mobility, never occurred to her. Stef felt a strong responsibility to go. Even with her body ravaged by the advance of her breast cancer, her spirit remained as indomitable as ever. She didn't have the strength to run or even to walk, so for this race, I would push her in a wheelchair.

The Race for the Cure always proved an emotional event for our family, as it is for everyone who participates. To see all the pink, to watch the tears of those who've beaten cancer or who run for someone afflicted by the disease, I could never look upon that and not feel changed. Every one of the participants embodies a fighting spirit. And for those too weak to take part, others do so in their honor to send the message, "I will fight for you." It's a beautiful testament to the human spirit.

Over the years, I felt touched and inspired across the spectrum of emotions at the Race for the Cure as Stef waged her battle, went into remission, then endured that cycle over and over again. I had watched Stef participate the first time with the triumphant mind-set of someone who'd beaten cancer, and then later with the determination of someone fighting cancer a second, third, and fourth time. Now she readied herself to participate with the unyielding approach of someone undeterred by the ravages of the disease.

I think we both knew, as we drove downtown that day, that this would be the final time we'd share the emotions of a Saturday morning at Race for the Cure. Stef wore a T-shirt and pink wig, like 6,000 others in the crowd of 40,000 participants, in honor of Heather Pick, a newscaster at WBNS-TV and a close friend. Heather and Stef shared many things in common, including a breast cancer diagnosis as young mothers. Heather died the previous November after a nine-year battle. Five years in, the cancer moved to Heather's spine and became inoperable. Now Stef knew her own cancer had lodged in the same place. Short of a miracle, she and I both knew what that meant.

Even so, as we neared the finish line that morning, Stef ordered me to stop pushing. She stood up from the wheelchair and, with Maddie's help, walked across the finish line. It was a defiant "in-your-face" to cancer, and a scene I instantly knew I needed to capture in my mind's eye. I resolved to cherish that memory of my unbelievably courageous wife and my oldest daughter, who inherited so many of her mom's amazing qualities. Noah, Macy, and Audrey engulfed their mom in hugs and tears. It gave us all a priceless moment we will never forget —a moment frozen forever in our hearts.

That unwavering spirit typified Stef's attitude throughout her battle. It sounds like hyperbole, but I truly never heard her complain once about having cancer. She never expressed bitterness when many of the patients she met over the years got cured and she didn't. Sue asked her one time, "Stef, with all you've done, do you ever ask, 'Why, Lord?'"

Stef just said, "I try not to."

Sue also asked her, "Do you ever get mad?"

Stef gave the same answer: "I try not to."

Knowing what loomed ahead of us in the coming months, I thought and prayed a lot about how to prepare Audrey and Macy for the worst. The number one thing I wanted to emphasize, not just with them but with everyone, centered on the eternal perspective both Stef and I had. We both knew the temporary nature of life on earth and that our real home awaits us in heaven. How could I get that through to a six-year-old and an eight-year-old on a level that they both could understand?

One day, one of our dogs started chewing on a baby bunny. That really upset the girls. I tried to comfort them by saying, "God created bunnies for a reason. If bunnies are good, then that bunny is in heaven now, and he doesn't have to worry anymore about a whacked-out poodle eating him. So now he's a happy bunny."

Stef usually handled those kinds of things with the kids and undoubtedly had a better way of relating on their level than I did. I typically took the tough-guy, linebacker approach to things. Whenever the kids fell and got hurt or cut themselves, I'd downplay the severity of it or call the injury a trophy. Macy hurt her wrist one day and I asked her, a little sarcastically, "Do you want me to take you to the hospital so we can put it in a cast?" The next day, we found out she really *had* broken her wrist. I felt like an idiot.

I couldn't be like that as much anymore. I realized I had to start transitioning in my approach. The cancer took away Stef's ability to be the mom she'd always been. She felt crappy all the time. She couldn't get her words out. She couldn't write. She needed help with just about everything. Just because she never complained didn't keep it from frustrating her. She felt extremely frustrated. She knew what to do, she just couldn't do it. Her body wouldn't allow it.

Once we reached that point, we had to learn to get enjoyment out of little things that had previously escaped our attention or we just took for granted. I gained pleasure from seeing her smile, or dress herself, or walk to the kitchen on her own. I talked to her about small wins. We considered it a win when she could stay out with her sisters for an hour longer. Attending one of the kids' events at school counted as another win.

A lot of my inspiration came from watching Stef's mom years before and seeing how she handled everything in the two years between her husband's seizure and when he died. She took such great care of him. I fell back on those memories as motivation for me in serving as caretaker for Stef. Those memories taught me something very valuable: Stef's mom demonstrated what I call "meaningful sacrifice," and I tried to duplicate that.

One of the things Stef loved to do as the cancer progressed was to take a bath. I'd draw her bath, get the different washcloths and lotions she liked, then make sure the water was the proper temperature. I'd get her in and out of the tub. I'd get down on my knees to dry off her feet, her legs, and the rest of her body. I'd get her pajamas laid out the way she wanted them.

The first time I did it, the nature of the moment reminded me of Christ washing the disciples' feet at the Last Supper. I thought about what a blessing I gained from being able to serve my wife in that manner. It humbled me to receive a very meaningful comfort from God amid the difficulty of seeing my wife so reliant on my assistance. That was an amazing gift He gave to me. It helped me tolerate the situation, without putting my fist through the wall.

CHAPTER 19

THE BLESSING
OF DISCOMFORT

I STRUGGLED TO CONTAIN MY FRUSTRATION AND HELPLESSNESS AS Stef's condition worsened over the summer. Little by little, her physical dexterity and mental capacity deteriorated. The chemo took a cumulative toll as it waged war against the cancer cells in her body. It felt like a piece of me eroded every day as I watched her slip slowly downhill. I can't imagine anything more heartbreaking than seeing someone you love go through such a lethal decline while you remain powerless to do anything about it.

In my football career, I always tried to prepare and practice so that nothing ever caught me off guard. But for more than ten years, always living with the possibility that something bad could happen to Stef, I could never escape the threat of cancer blind-siding our family. If she had a cough, what did that mean? If she had an ache or a pain, what did that mean? I couldn't figure out a way to conquer that uncertainty and fear.

God gave me the push I needed with my vision of the neon sign the morning after we learned the cancer had spread to her spine and spinal fluid. Hearing Him tell me, "No matter what, Chris, everything is going to be OK. Trust me," motivated me to do what I needed to do in order to avoid getting caught by surprise again. He gave me the strength to explain the situation to Maddie and Noah and to begin to formulate a plan to help us move forward if we didn't get the miracle we continued to seek.

I leaned on one of my favorite verses: "[The Lord said,] 'My grace is sufficient for you, for my power is made perfect in weakness.' Therefore I will boast all the more gladly about my weaknesses, so that Christ's power may rest on me" (2 Corinthians 12:9). I hung my hat on that assurance. I didn't relish coming up with a plan of action for the immediate future, but I drew strength from some giants of the faith who also had battled fear in their lives. When God asked Moses to lead the Israelites out of bondage, he responded with doubt, asking, "What can I do?" He feared the mandate God gave him. Jonah ran away from God. Gideon had to put out a fleece twice before he became willing to lead the battle against the Midianites.

I realized that God probably wouldn't take away all my anxiety, but He would equip me not to walk in fear. The fear I had lived with for so many years didn't overwhelm me anymore. It no longer hung over my shoulder as a constant companion.

Ever since Stef's battle began, I'd disciplined myself to think like a football player: *Positive thoughts. Positive thoughts.* As a player, you never want to think about *What if we lose?* But you do think, *If something doesn't work, we have to find something else. If this happens, what do we do?* I needed to equip myself to respond under pressure in *this* situation. If I couldn't do that, I would do no one any good. If I couldn't think and react clearly, then I wouldn't help Stef or our children. I looked at everything as a team endeavor, and I didn't want to let my team down. If anything caught me off guard, without a plan, then I might let my team down.

I'd always admired the parenting skills of Sue and Bill as they raised four girls, two in college and two in high school. So one day I had a conversation with Sue and asked her to help me raise my girls if the time came. If Stef couldn't do it, I needed someone's help. Initiating that conversation hurt a lot. It forced me essentially to admit that Stef wouldn't survive, and it forced me to admit my shortcomings as a father. Still, it had to be done for the good of my family.

As I contemplated the increasing possibility of Stef's death, I had to face my own inability to attend to all the things a girl needs as she grows up. I had confidence I could identify my son's needs, but

I didn't grow up around girls. I didn't have any sisters. I had almost nothing in common with girls. I didn't have any close female friends. I knew that eventually I would need the perspective of a woman and a mother. I didn't know how to shop for girls. Makeup tips? I had no idea. Menstrual cycles? No idea. Hair? Whenever I tried to do it, it looked terrible.

But just as it works with a well-functioning team, Maddie stepped in and really excelled. It amazed me to watch her get Audrey and Macy ready for church. She helped them brush their teeth and braided their hair so they looked just perfect. Maddie really responded and, I think, enjoyed taking command of the things she felt led to do. I'd hear her giggling with the girls. That was music to my soul.

Even in the midst of great despair, God kept feeding me when I needed it most. I held on tightly to the little daily snippets of joy that came from hearing my kids' laughter. Their resilience lifted me as they persevered amid the sorrow we all felt. Watching them go about their lives, pushing through the adversity, and adjusting to our new normal made me feel good about how they accepted our parenting instruction over the years.

Having that conversation with Sue completed a big part of the plan I would need to put into action if Stef didn't recover. I checked our will and brought it up to date. I met with our financial adviser to eliminate any surprises there. I contacted some people at school to make sure they were watching my kids' emotions and behavior. I conferred with someone I trusted about the proper way to notify the media and the public if Stef passed away. After checking all those things off my list, I relaxed just a little. I knew I had prepared as much as possible, but I knew I could never get prepared enough to lose my one and only love.

Ever since Stef's first diagnosis, and every year since then, people often asked her or me to call someone or visit someone struggling with a serious illness. Most of the time, it involved someone in a terminal situation, often from cancer. Doing that forced me well beyond my comfort zone, but I always seemed to perform better when I didn't feel comfortable.

I received one of those calls the summer when Stef struggled in the aftermath of radiation and during chemo on her brain and spine. I had met this guy just once, and I didn't even remember him. He told me about a man at The James who had cancer. He said this man's neighbor had expressed concern about his salvation, especially since he seemed to have a bleak future. Would I visit him and witness to him? I got the call at home and thought, *Dude, don't you understand what I have going on in my own life? Why are you calling me?* At that time, with Stef's condition deteriorating, I had a whole list of things to take care of before I could even leave the house. I didn't have the luxury of just popping out whenever I wanted to go someplace. But I told the guy to call me later and I would try to make it work.

A day or two later, Stef and I attended a concert at our church. The music's spiritual message touched Stef very deeply and she started crying. I thought about the guy who requested that I speak to his friend at The James. He hadn't called back, so I planned to blow it off. I figured he had gotten the message that I didn't want to do it. But God really convicted me: *What are you doing? I put that call in your life for a reason. I realize it's out of your comfort zone. That has nothing to do with anything.* All of that went through my mind during the concert.

That night, as soon as we returned home, I called the guy and told him to meet me at The James at noon the next day, a Sunday. We went up to the room and met the cancer patient, a fireman from northern Ohio. I found out the nurses had delayed his release by a couple of hours, which made him angry. He wanted out of there, and I didn't blame him. He and I talked, with his wife and family in the room. We talked about cancer, about living with it and the roller-coaster ride of emotions. We talked about how it affects a person spiritually and what he relied on from a spiritual point of view. We talked about everything for about an hour and then said our good-byes. We had had an emotional conversation.

When I walked out, I realized God does not always want me in a comfort zone. He provides comfort zones, but when the time comes to accomplish His work—dealing with cancer and helping others deal with cancer—it will never be easy for me. The only way I can handle it is through His strength. I'm at my best if I rely on that. I can't do anything alone.

God provides everything I need in those situations. I'm not allowed to rest in a comfort zone when it comes to cancer. My experiences and the lessons I've learned from doing things right and from doing things wrong have convinced me the whole thing—Stef's battle and what it mushroomed into for us publicly—resulted from God's master plan for our lives.

With most things, the more you do them, the easier they become. But these speaking requests grew more difficult for me over the years because the challenges grew more difficult. What could I possibly say to the emails, the phone calls, the person in the hospital bed I'd never met? I came to believe that God must speak through me in those situations if I approached it humbly and relied on Him.

It sometimes felt like a curse, but I've come to embrace it as a gift —that people feel enough of an attachment to give me an avenue into their lives. I consider it an honor that they want to hear what I have to say or think that I can help them. I take that responsibility very, very seriously. I understand the gravity of it when I go into those situations, and I'm glad to have that honor. None of that makes it easy, but still I'm glad that God gives me these opportunities.

I suppose I knew when we went public with Stef's diagnosis that this could happen, but I didn't expect the story to explode like it did. Being in the public eye brings both positives and negatives. When someone wants me to minister to another person in emotional pain, to offer a spiritual perspective to someone who may have no interest in God, or to tell about the peace and joy I have as a believer in Christ, I see no negatives to that. It's all positive, but also very challenging. I feel what they feel. I take on their pain, their suffering, their sadness. It brings everything back to me. And when I get done serving in that way, it often ends up being therapeutic, not just for others but for me as well.

Most of the time, those situations go well. But sometimes, I don't make a connection with the other person. Sometimes I leave not knowing if I made a difference. I've learned not to concern myself with that. Maybe I'm not supposed to know the answer right away. I once talked to a man over the phone who seemed very sad. His wife had cancer, and I felt his deep sadness and that of his family. I felt as though I had let him down. I couldn't make him feel better. The competitor in me took that truth very hard. I felt very disappointed.

Before I speak with anybody about these situations, I read 1 Peter 3:15, which says, "Always be prepared to give an answer to everyone who asks you to give the reason for the hope that you have. But do this with gentleness and respect." Taking my cue from that verse, I don't come out and punch people in the head with the Bible. I usually ask something like, "How do you cope with this?" If they ask me the same question, then I make reference to the gospel. I believe with all my heart in the hope mentioned in 1 Peter 3:15. That hope is a guarantee, not a wish, and I always approach it that way. Now, do I always see results? No. I don't think I'll see the results until I get to heaven. Maybe then, God will show me.

Stef and I always considered it an honor to serve people in this way, even when the cancer began to slowly overtake her. We often said that cancer gave us so many blessings in our life, and that those blessings outnumbered the heartaches. That viewpoint became clearer to us as the cards, emails, and calls accumulated as more and more people learned about Stef's condition. After she skipped the Champions luncheon and after Maddie helped her across the finish line at Race for the Cure, the word got out.

People from Stef's youth through her adult years encouraged her by referring to the courage and grace she had shown and how that had touched them. They gave us a glimpse into the ripple effect of her battle. Her contentment, her positive outlook, her faith—all those things still radiated from her even as the cancer advanced. Stef's actions in the midst of dying gave a powerful testimony about the source of the peace that sustained her. The true beauty of my wife's witness to the transforming power of Jesus Christ as her savior showed up in the unique way she exposed her faith to everyone without imposing it on anyone. You couldn't know her even a little bit and not get that message loud and clear.

CHAPTER 20

CELEBRATING LIFE

WHEN SHE SAID IT THE FIRST TIME, I THOUGHT STEF CAME UP WITH her directive about "no doom and gloom" spontaneously, the day we planned her memorial service at the hospital. I grew to understand that she didn't just pull that phrase out of the air, but had committed to living by that philosophy long ago. She obviously had thought a lot over the years about how, if worse came to worst, she wanted her final months to play out. So as spring turned to summer in 2009, she enlisted her sisters and mom to help her continue doing what she'd done since cancer first struck in 1998. Back then, and throughout her battle, Stef had made it clear through her actions that she wouldn't allow cancer to dictate to her. She resolved to live life on her terms.

When the first clumps of her hair began to fall out from the initial doses of chemo, she decided to shave her head before treatment made all her hair fall out. She wanted a large family when we first got married, and neither breast cancer at age thirty nor a Stage IV diagnosis at age thirty-two deterred her from doubling the number of children we had before she got sick. Once she committed to participating in every Race for the Cure, not even the ravages of radiation and chemo could keep her from getting out of her wheelchair and crossing the finish line.

Stef's fighting spirit just wouldn't permit her to yield, even when her body became progressively weaker. She wouldn't simply endure what loomed as her final months of life; she squeezed every drop out of every day. She didn't want to stay in bed and have the kids

167

remember her that way. She wanted to be a part of everything, and she wanted everything as normal as possible.

"No doom and gloom" wasn't just a phrase. She made it her mantra. She would say those words whenever a conversation turned too serious or a moment became too tinged with emotion. She recognized that her time on earth was ebbing away each day. But for her, that meant a call to action, not inaction. "I cannot survive this way," she told Sue one day when resting in bed, feeling particularly lousy from treatment. "I don't want to live the rest of my life in this dark room."

Ever the big sister, Sue came to the rescue. She made a list of fun things Stef could do with her, Sandy, and their mom, Myra, while they rotated helping our family take care of Stef every day. Sue posted the list on our refrigerator. Without fail, every night before she went to bed, Stef would ask, "What's the plan for tomorrow?"

Even with cancer relentlessly attacking her brain and spine, she became so energized by the urgency of living life to its fullest that she nearly wore out her sisters and her mom. Sue scrambled to come up with new things for them to do. At times, they all needed a second wind to keep pace with Stef's desire to get out and go.

The Belcher girls lived a new adventure every day. They went shopping whenever they couldn't think of anything else, but they also found plenty of other things to keep Stef engaged. Right after school let out in June, our family, Sue's family, and Myra went to Cedar Point Amusement Park. Despite the cold and rainy weather, Stef had a blast watching the kids ride the roller coasters. About ten days later, on a Saturday night, we were almost ready to leave for a Christopher Cross concert when I felt a sharp pain in my abdomen. At the emergency room, the pain went away almost as fast as it had appeared. I had passed a kidney stone—and just in time too. We barely made it for the start of the concert. I teased Stef and Sue about how some people say passing a kidney stone is the closest thing to the pain of childbirth. "I've got to tell you, ladies, it wasn't that big of a deal." Stef called that night "the best thing all summer," probably because the music reminded her of the carefree times in high school before cancer struck her father.

As the summer progressed, and as her strength diminished, Stef lamented the increasing loss of her independence. For a person who'd always been on the go, she found it hard to rely on others to get around. "If only I could drive," Stef said to Sue a couple times. That gave Sue an idea. The girls had given their mom a three-wheeled bicycle, but Myra never really used it. "What if we get Mom's bike and you can ride that?" Sue asked.

Stef hesitated at first, probably because trying and failing would have added one more limitation to the list of things she couldn't do. But Sue kept encouraging her, and Stef gradually warmed to the idea. When the sun came out on one of the first really beautiful days of the summer, Sue told her, "Today is the day. We're going to get you on that bike."

One of our neighbors happened to be watching as Sue helped Stef onto the three-wheeler, and she began pedaling. Stef sensed a long overdue feeling of freedom and independence with every revolution of the pedals. Sue walked along beside her as they passed the first city block. "Can we keep going?" Stef asked. They passed another block, and another, eventually riding past Noah's middle school. Whenever Stef veered a bit off course, Sue would gently adjust the handlebars. A look of pure joy spread across Stef's face as she pedaled, turning her head and looking at everything. She drank in the beauty of the day with the wonderment of a person set free from bondage.

The neighbor who saw them that day wrote Sue a note:

Emotion flooded as I watched the two of you for only a few seconds. Such a strange mix of feelings for me. It must be overwhelming for you at times. I felt sad, while the picture was so beautiful to me. I'm sure I will never forget it. [We] are so grateful to God to know you and Stef, your husbands and your family. For us, you live as people from another planet, citizens of "no ordinary country"; a glorious thing to see.

Stef's passion for life often touched something in people that stirred long-dormant emotions. She could, with the very nature of the way she lived, put people in touch with feelings that pulled meaning from things they'd otherwise ignore.

In all the years of our marriage, and even when we dated in high school and college, I never lost sight of the privilege of being part of her life. To watch her press on against all the difficulty she faced and yet maintain such a can-do spirit both humbled and amazed me. Her motivation came from her faith, first of all, but also from those whom she knew would watch closely how she reacted. As she said to an interviewer in 2006: "A goal of mine has always been to set a good example for my kids while facing this disease. I want them to know they can make lemonade from lemons, no matter what challenges their lives may have. I want them to see me as a strong woman, who fights this disease bravely ... knowing ultimately that my life is in God's hands."

Now that she'd mastered the three-wheel bike, Stef wanted to make more "lemonade." She enlisted Sue to take her grocery shopping three days after their first cycling adventure. Stef hadn't shopped for groceries in about six months. Radiation had torched her taste buds to the point where nothing tasted good to her, but everything still looked good to her. Sue helped her into one of those motorized scooters for handicapped people. Once Stef took the controls, she flashed back to her childhood and the moped she loved riding full throttle. Sue could hardly keep up with her as Stef sped down the aisles, pointing to what Sue should grab for their cart. Stef became so preoccupied, she almost drove smack into a huge store display of hundreds of items.

She attacked everything as a new and invigorating experience. Her enthusiasm made us all understand how much we overlooked every day. She brought a childlike joy to whatever she did, despite her grave illness. Watching her "soldier on" ingrained an unforgettable lesson in living that provided us a host of treasured memories.

As a young girl, Stef loved horses, and she passed along that love to Maddie. After we bought Maddie a new horse that summer, Stef insisted on making the trip to Delaware, a city about thirty miles away, to watch Maddie compete for the first time in a jumping competition. We visited the Columbus Zoo for a behind-the-scenes tour. And we had a blast at our Spielman Scramble golf outing, designed to raise money for Stef's fund. She piled into the cart with me, Sandy,

Sue, and Myra for a wild, bumpy ride around the course. It felt so good to laugh as a family.

Everything she did revolved around her goal of making lasting memories, so it didn't surprise me when Stef poured herself into celebrating our twentieth anniversary on June 24. She always cherished our times together at the cabin we owned in the Hideaway Hills near Athens, about fifty miles away. Stef woke up at 7:30 that morning, which was very early for her, given how she felt at the time. It touched me to see how much effort she put into making the day special for me. She had bought a new dress on one of her shopping trips with her sisters. She put it on, along with a new set of earrings, and got ready to go before I even left the house for some broadcasting commitments that morning. Myra, Sue, and one of Sue's daughters, Lauren, drove to our cabin, decorated it, and set the table for a special dinner that night. By the time I got home around three, Stef's energy had all but evaporated, but she wouldn't hear of not going. After dinner, because she felt totally exhausted, we just went to bed and returned home the next day. It touched me to see how much of a priority she placed on our little celebration. She obviously wanted to spend some time together in the place where we'd enjoyed so many special memories.

Less than two weeks later, on July 4, Stef returned to the cabin for a family movie night. We watched one of my favorite movies, *Rocky*, which seemed appropriate for the opponent we faced.

Stef mustered some of that prizefighter's spirit in late July, surprising everyone at Vacation Bible School at our church, Trinity United Methodist. Stef had choreographed the big wrap-up performance every year, but lacked the strength to do that again. Instead, Sue took Stef to church in the wheelchair every day so she could watch the kids practice their singing and dancing. Then on the final day, Stef mustered the strength to get out of her chair and walk to the front so she could sing, dance, and do the hand motions for each song with the kids. Few adults who witnessed that scene left with dry eyes.

As the summer continued to unfold, Stef kept showing me the power a person can summon when motivated to persevere. By her birthday on July 18, her leg function had deteriorated significantly.

After we came home from dinner, we put on some Michael Jackson music and it energized Stef, almost as if she were back in high school. She loved Michael Jackson music. She could moonwalk, do the robot, all of it. The louder the music played that night, the more she got into it. Before long she got up from her chair, pointing and moving as best she could.

Those times of laughter and celebration—though special and cherished—provided only a momentary respite amid the months of restricted mobility Stef endured. She could walk down our stairs, but she had to crawl to go back up. I eventually had to lift her left leg and bend it for her to walk up the stairs. At times, the heartache nearly overwhelmed me. My jaw would tighten and I'd struggle to breathe. It hurt so much to see the limitations on her motor skills inflicted by the advancing cancer. But God gave me the strength not to show her or the kids how much it affected me. Stef had issued a strict order, "No doom and gloom." And I remained committed to following that order.

CHAPTER 21

TELL ME LIKE
THE DOCTOR TOLD YOU

I STRUGGLED TO FULLY ENJOY SOME OF THE LIGHTER MOMENTS OF the summer because I knew one of the toughest parts in my plan of action remained unfinished. I'd covered my bases in every area but the one I didn't yet have the wisdom to complete. At some point, I would have to bring Macy and Audrey, our two youngest children, in on the painful reality ahead of us. We always held out hope for a miracle, but I had to deal in reality too, and the worst possible reality became more and more likely as the months went on.

The responsibility to prepare Macy and Audrey for what lay ahead of us as a family weighed on me tremendously. Stef had passed the point of being able to join me in having such a conversation. Mentally, she lacked the sharpness required because of the chemo attacking her brain cells.

I prayed hard for wisdom, but I felt no leading to proceed. I decided to wait for that prompting before doing or saying anything. I believed God was protecting the girls by limiting their interaction with Stef as her condition worsened. Other than when we did something fun as a family, they spent very little time with her. They were so active, and Stef spent many hours resting upstairs. Yet each evening, she would always see them to give a hug and goodnight kiss. Maybe God used that diminished contact to soften the blow for Macy and Audrey. Perhaps He used it to answer my prayers that they be guarded and protected.

I took some comfort from the fact that I wouldn't be completely alone whenever the conversation with the girls took place. I trusted God to give me the right words. Macy and Audrey obviously knew their mom had some serious health issues, and they felt sad about that. But I think they benefitted from a God-given protection for little ones who have a hard time comprehending the gravity of life-and-death situations.

I certainly could have used some similar protection myself. Nothing could prepare me to lose, in the prime of her life, the woman I loved. Both Stef and I knew we would see each other again in heaven, where cancer could not follow. Still, it crushed me to contemplate letting go of someone I loved so much, someone who had been a part of my life since my junior year of high school. I knew it would devastate the kids, and it also crushed Stef to think about what she would miss in our children's lives. High school proms, graduations, weddings, grandchildren—all the things you look forward to celebrating as a family, she wouldn't get to experience. Our kids wouldn't get to have her as part of those landmark events. We knew the worst of heaven would be better than the best of earth, but that didn't eliminate the enormous pain right around the corner.

Stef's MRIs and scans had held pretty steady throughout the summer, but we hadn't seen any improvement to indicate that she would rally and improve. At best, the treatment had held her cancer at bay. But the disease often advances and activates without warning, until waging one last overwhelming strike. Stef enjoyed a reasonable quality of life, but it had become clear that she would make no comeback to her old self as she had so many times before.

Some would hide from public view in that situation, but Stef never grew ashamed or uncomfortable with people seeing her in her limited condition. Some people pitied her, which is a natural human emotion, but she never pitied herself. She felt a responsibility to show others that she didn't fear death. She focused on enjoying the moment and enjoying the day.

Stef got really excited when I learned that in my first assignment for ESPN that fall I would cover Ohio State's opener against the Naval

Academy. Earlier that summer, the College Football Hall of Fame named me to its class of 2009 inductees. Typically, I didn't get too excited about awards. I'd won my share over the years, but none of them meant as much to me as the success of our teams. This award, though, meant a lot because I knew Stef wanted it for me. She celebrated when the Hall of Fame announcement came down, and she celebrated even more when Ohio State offered to recognize my induction in an on-field ceremony on September 5. I didn't know if I could attend, because I didn't normally broadcast many Ohio State games. But maybe some divine intervention took place, because when my schedule came out, the network assigned me to OSU's home opener. If the school had chosen a date later that fall, Stef probably couldn't have made it. But that day, she still had the strength to attend, along with Maddie, Noah, Macy, and Audrey. Walking onto the field before a crowd of more than 100,000 scared Macy and Audrey a bit. I just told them, "This is a once-in-a-lifetime opportunity for our family. You don't have an option. You're going." Noah and Maddie knew the drill. They got excited about it for their mom's sake and mine.

On the day of the game, OSU took care of getting them all down to the field. I met them there after working the first half for ESPN from the television booth in the press box. I pushed Stef out onto the field in her wheelchair and the kids followed. Ohio State did a nice video presentation on the scoreboard and read off some of my career achievements, but I didn't see or hear any of that. I focused my attention on soaking up every mental picture I could of the kids and Stef.

When they announced my name, the crowd roared and Stef began pumping her left arm and waving her fist in the air. The fans rose and gave us a standing ovation. With all my heart, I believe the fans directed their applause more toward her than me. I believe that because afterward every comment I received referred to Stefanie and the courage she showed going out there. She earned that ovation because she always had proven herself the toughest warrior in our family.

I hoped that those who witnessed that scene realized where we stood with our faith. Even though we faced a difficult situation, God had given us the strength. None of that came from my power or Stef's ability to endure tough circumstances. The strength came from God. Stef always said that when she prayed, she rarely received what she asked for, but she always received what she needed. I think I got what I needed that day on the field in Ohio Stadium.

Ever since we first started walking the cancer road in July 1998, we felt a spiritual strength fortifying us time and again. Sometimes it came through Bible reading or study. Sometimes it came through a song, a prayer that really connected, a card in the mail, or a call from someone we knew. We always seemed to get exactly what we needed just when we needed it. Some of those times came on Sunday nights that fall, when neighbors and friends gathered at Miller Park in Upper Arlington for a prayer vigil. The community came together to show its love and concern for both Stef and Blake Haxton, a UA High School rower who required almost twenty surgeries to survive an attack of flesh-eating bacteria that claimed one of his legs up to the hip and the other to well above the knee.

The vigils had no rehearsed program or agenda, but offered some amazing, uplifting moments as people united in support of others battling the most difficult of circumstances. Not everyone who attended shared a belief in Christ. Even so, they came to lend their emotional support. Everyone there heard the gospel as the source of each family's ability to persevere. I pushed Stef to the park for one candlelight vigil, and I spoke at a couple of others. We didn't attend every week, but just knowing a prayer vigil was happening every Sunday night gave us a boost at a time when we really needed it.

The day-to-day heavy lifting around the house still fell to Sue and Sandy. One or both spent every day with Stef. We can never repay the debt of gratitude we owe them. I did my best to try to make sure our children understood the enormous blessing of having people who loved us and sacrificed so much for us. One night after coming home from Bible study, I gathered the kids around me and read from 1 Corinthians 13:4–8: "Love is patient, love is kind. It does not envy, it does not boast, it is not proud. It does not dishonor others, it is not self-seeking, it is not easily angered, it keeps no record of wrongs. Love does not delight in evil but rejoices with the truth. It always protects, always trusts, always hopes, always perseveres. Love never fails."

I asked the kids, "Who in our life does this passage remind you of?"

Right away, the two older ones said, "Aunt Sandy and Aunt Sue." They realized the tremendous sacrifice both had made.

Sue and her family lived about five minutes away from us. She became a rock on whom we leaned over the years, and not just when Stef's health took a pronounced turn for the worse in March. Although Sue often accompanied Stef to her doctor appointments, she expressed some hesitance about going along on October 6. Audrey had a dance class that day and really wanted me to come, so Sue put aside her uneasiness and agreed to take Stef in for her scans. Some recent warning signs—Stef had trouble walking and her mental confusion had increased—put us more than a little on edge over what this scan might reveal.

Sue asked me to call the doctors and request that they not say anything about the results in front of her. She believed strongly that only Stef and I should discuss those issues. Sue didn't want to be a part of that or be there to hear a dire prognosis. As much as we'd leaned on Sue over the years, and as much as she had been a rock for our family, Stef was still Sue's little sister. I certainly understood why it would be so difficult for Sue to hear such devastating news.

Stef's chemo drip had robbed her of the ability to fully understand anything the doctors might have told her. She just submitted to the tests and then came home with Sue. Dr. Cavaliere called me while I was still watching Audrey's dance class. He told me the numbers didn't appear promising. I knew what that meant. The cancer had advanced. It had come out of its holding pattern. The chemo could stave it off no longer.

I processed the gut-punch of that news and instantly refocused on Audrey and her dancing. I tried to pay attention as my mind raced. Later, as we drove home, I chatted with Audrey about her dance class and tried not to let on about what I now knew.

Stef and Sue were waiting for us at home. Sue took Audrey into another room and I took Stef into the living room. "I have to talk to you."

"Should I be scared?" she asked.

"Yes. Because I am."

I told her about the tests and that Dr. Cavaliere recommended we stop treatment. I looked very intently into her eyes. "Stef, this is not a decision that I can make. This is a decision that only you can make."

She had fought too long, too hard, and too courageously for me to declare an end to her battle. The best-case scenario for additional treatment would buy her only a short amount of time. The doctor didn't see the merit in it and neither did I, but Stef would have to make that choice for herself.

She sat for a bit and didn't say anything. Then she looked at me and said, "What did we just talk about?" The relaxation medicine she had taken for her scans that day and the cumulative effect of chemotherapy kept her from focusing on the gravity of our conversation.

It tore me up to tell her the news the first time. Now I had to repeat it. "It's growing in your brain. The doctors think we should stop treatment, but that's up to you."

She sat there quietly, thinking about what I had said. A minute or two later she asked, "What did the doctor say?"

It felt surreal, having a conversation I never wanted to have even once, and having it over and over. I repeated it a third time, and this time she understood.

"Tell me the rest," she said. "Tell me like the doctor told you."

I explained again about the one last chemo option—that it would buy her only a month, if that, which the doctor didn't recommend.

"What do you want to do?" I asked.

She thought for just a bit and said, "I'm tired of fighting."

"OK," I said. "That's OK."

Then she had something else to tell me.

"I don't want any doom and gloom. No doom and gloom around here."

Telling Stef the horrible news took a tremendous toll on me, but I couldn't stop now.

Maddie and Noah needed to know too. I dreaded telling them, but putting it off wouldn't make it any easier. Stef and I always had been honest with them on a level they could understand. Now I owed them the truth, even if the truth would devastate them. So that night, I spoke to each of them individually, describing honestly the bleak nature of Stef's prognosis. Then I got them together with me in Maddie's room. "Guys, this is what you need to do. This is what I do. The first thing: Do not crawl, walk, or jog to God. You run to God for peace and strength. Number two: Trust your instincts. Both of you have the Holy Spirit in your hearts. He will guide you in the decisions you make. Rely on that. Trust in that. And number three: Honor your mother in everything you do."

We cried. We hugged. We cried some more. They said good-night and we said a prayer. I then prayed a prayer of thanksgiving for my children.

I thought about what had just happened. I wrote down my three main points on two pieces of paper so they each would have it as a reference, and then I added one last sentence for each of them. For Maddie: "All you have to do is be Maddie, Stef's daughter." And for Noah: "All you have to do is be Noah, Stef's son." I signed each note, "I love you, Dad."

I wanted to emphasize that they already had been doing the right things. I wanted to remind them who they are and whose they are. I couldn't have felt prouder about how they'd handled the situation to that point, and I had confidence they would do well in the weeks ahead. I knew it would be hard on them, but I took comfort in knowing that God promises to equip believers in Christ with the ability to withstand whatever challenges He allows in their lives. This would be a massive challenge, for me and for them. But we had the shared love and strength of each other, and we had the love and strength we shared in Christ to get us through.

Whenever tough news had come our way, Maddie and Noah had proven themselves resilient. They faced an array of heartaches that most young people never have to endure. I couldn't anticipate how they might respond, but now that the moment had arrived, I couldn't have felt more gratified with their response.

They continued to function well under extreme circumstances, with honor and great courage. It amazed me to watch them show such tremendous maturity beyond their years. I believed that, in the long run, surviving this ordeal would fortify their character.

Many times I asked God for mercy for my children. I always thought He would grant my request through healing Stefanie. Instead, He answered it through the comfort He gave the kids and me throughout the whole process, and through the peace of mind He granted to Stef.

I turned forty-four on the following Sunday, October 11. One of our family traditions had always been a visit to Circle S Farms in Grove City for its Fall Festival. We made the trip on a day that couldn't have been more sunny and beautiful. Maddie and Noah never let on that anything was wrong. Audrey and Macy had as much fun as ever. Stef enjoyed watching them run and play and laugh and pick out their pumpkins for jack-o-lanterns. All in all, we had a great day; but even the good times now came with a bittersweet side, knowing what we faced.

Times like that sometimes left me feeling like an actor, playing a part. Inside, I had this horrible feeling of dread because I knew Macy and Audrey still needed to know the full story of their mom's condition. Outwardly, I tried to be a fun daddy, enjoying their youthful exuberance. The conflict of those emotions nagged at me. But I still didn't feel led by the Holy Spirit to have that conversation. I had questioned a lot of things over the years, but I'd learned never to question God's timing. I never wavered in believing He would put the burden on my heart, along with the right words to say to my youngest girls, when it suited His schedule, not mine. Reading verses like Isaiah 40:31 only strengthened my belief: "Those who hope in the LORD will renew their strength. They will soar on wings like eagles; they will run and not grow weary, they will walk and not be faint." I chose to wait because I knew that in my own strength, I could not tell Macy and Audrey as gently and effectively as I could if I waited for the Lord's leading.

That leading finally came about three weeks later, around 6 a.m. on Friday, October 30, as I prepared to board a flight to Chicago. I don't know why it hit me then, but it did. I felt an overwhelming necessity to have the conversation after I returned from working the Penn State–Northwestern game in Evanston, Illinois.

Knowing the time had come didn't lift the burden over what I should say. I didn't know what a seven- and eight-year-old could understand. I thought and prayed about it all weekend. One thing I knew: I wanted Maddie and Noah in the room with me. Those two had really stepped up in taking care of their sisters since Stef's condition worsened in March. So when I returned home Sunday morning, I got my two oldest off to the side and said, "Tonight, we're going to tell Audrey and Macy what's going on."

The rest of the day, I just watched the clock tick down. I felt nervous about how they would react because Macy had really struggled when Stef got sick. It concerned me how she would handle *this* horrible news. I had no idea how Audrey would react. Finally, the time came to have the conversation. I got them together and said, "I need to talk to you."

"About what?" Macy asked.

"It's about Mom."

"Is she going to be OK?"

"That's what I need to talk to you about."

Whenever Macy got nervous, she had to go to the bathroom. She excused herself and then came back walking slowly, as if sensing what I was about to tell them.

I put an arm around each one of them and said, "Mace, Aud, Mommy isn't going to get any better."

They started crying. They weren't inconsolable, but the news profoundly affected them. I think, in their hearts, they knew this was coming.

Then I said, "But there is one way she can get better. When she gets to heaven, she's going to get a whole new body. She's going to get to do the things that she loves to do. You know, Mom loves to run. She loves to dance. She loves to play. She'll get to do all those things she loves to do, and she won't ever have to worry about being sick again. That's something we should be very, very happy about."

Audrey asked, "Is her hair going to grow back?"

"Yeah," I said, "it's going to be more beautiful than you ever remember it, because she's going to get a new body that can never be hurt again. God is going to give her that."

Macy asked, "Is she going to get to see her dad?"

"I think her dad will be waiting for her," I said. "Isn't that going to make Mom happy?"

They both agreed it would, yet both remained upset. As I tried to calm them, I prayed that each one would receive the gift of perseverance.

Macy finally said, "Dad, can I go up into your room and watch baseball?"

Audrey was still crying when she and Macy went into Stef's room and gave her a hug.

A little while later, I had to drive Noah to meet a friend. Before we left, I checked on Macy upstairs and then went looking for Audrey. I couldn't find her. I called her name a few times until she answered.

"I'm down here in the basement," she said. "I'm with Maddie."

"What are you doing?" I asked.

"Crying my eyes out."

CHAPTER 22

PINK ROSES AND
PRECIOUS MEMORIES

I ACTUALLY FELT RELIEF OVER AUDREY'S AND MACY'S REACTION TO hearing the hard truth about Stef's condition. I knew by the tone of their voices that they understood the gravity of what we had discussed. I couldn't and didn't expect it not to hurt. *Of course* it hurt. We all hurt, but now we had no secrets from each other. Everyone knew where we stood.

That night, Macy and Audrey wanted to sleep in my bed. They wanted their dad close to them, and I couldn't say no. For some time Stef had been staying in a hospital bed in a different room. With everything on my mind, and with two little urchins wiggling around all night, I didn't sleep well. About 4:30 a.m., I got out of bed and took a walk around the house. I felt a tinge of guilt. I realized, now that I had told our little ones, I was ready for Stef to die.

The only thing left was for Stef to get the eternal rest and relief she so richly deserved. Each day, she had slipped a little more downhill. She hadn't eaten in more than two weeks. I'd asked Dr. Shapiro whether he believed Stefanie could hang on until Christmas. He told me he couldn't make a prediction, because a cancer patient motivated by a personal goal can live far beyond what their scans and test results suggest.

I tried to imagine what Stef's goal might be. She had spoken to me about wanting to attend a ceremony December 10 at the Waldorf

Astoria for the College Football Hall of Fame inductees. "What if I'm not well enough to go to New York?" she asked me.

"Then I won't go," I said.

"Yes, you will," she said, pounding the table for emphasis.

Given her condition, she couldn't possibly make that trip now. She had to know that, so I thought maybe she'd set her sights on watching Noah play the lead in *High School Musical* the first weekend in November at Jones Middle School. Stef had choreographed the school's production the year before, drawing on her dance background. She took Macy and Audrey with her to practice every night. The little girls thoroughly enjoyed themselves. Being around a theatrical production put Stef back in her element, creating and directing like she did on her television show in Detroit. She savored every minute of that time with Noah and the girls. Now, just a year later, I didn't know if she could sit upright for two hours to watch, let alone focus on the stage performance.

Stef's sister Cindy arrived from California the weekend of the show, which brought all four sisters together. I asked Sue if she thought Stef could go to the play and sit through it. Before she could answer, Sandy said, "We have to get her to that play." The teachers in charge knew about Stef's deteriorating condition, so they videotaped Noah's dress rehearsal in case Stef couldn't go. But as we discussed whether to attempt it, Stef sat up in bed for the first time in more than a week and said, "Get me my wheelchair. I want to go out to the kitchen."

"Why?" I asked.

"Because I need to practice sitting up for the play tonight," she said.

"Are you sure that's a good idea?" I asked.

She proceeded to show me just how good of an idea it was. She sat there for two solid hours, demonstrating her resolve. So I figured, "Why not?"

Sue's husband, Bill, and I got Stef from the house into the car and from the car into the auditorium. The staff at the school really came through. They set up a place for her wheelchair in the front row.

Other than with God's strength, I don't know how she did it. But Stef sat there for the entire performance and never wavered. She gazed at Noah the entire time, completely engaged. You could see how much effort that took, but she did it without faltering. It was so incredibly cool to watch. We all felt so thankful Noah got to savor that memory and share it with his mom.

The next day, Sunday morning, brought some fantastic weather, very warm and sunny for early November. Stef woke up and said, "I'm going again." This time, I didn't doubt her determination at all.

We got the entire family together, and I pushed her wheelchair through the neighborhood to the school for the afternoon matinee performance. Noah did his thing again, and she watched every second of it.

Afterward, they had a big bouquet of pink roses for Noah to present to Stef as a way of honoring her for helping them throughout the years. He came over, wearing this huge smile, and hugged and kissed his mom. Everyone stood and applauded. Noah was crying. We all were crying. I'll cherish that priceless moment forever.

Noah shared the lead in the play with one of his friends, Danny Hummer. Danny played the lead on Friday and Noah did the lead on Saturday and Sunday. Danny started walking toward the stage right before everyone dispersed and Stef saw him. She grabbed him and pulled him down close to her in her wheelchair.

"You're a good friend to Noah," she said in Danny's ear.

Given the noise in the auditorium and the weakness in Stef's voice, Danny struggled to hear what she said. He asked her to repeat it.

"Be a good friend to Noah," she said.

Exhausted, riddled with cancer, Stef still made sure, first and foremost, to look out for her son—a mom to the very end.

We continued to ride that high for a few days until Stef insisted that she and her sisters and their mom have another girls' night out. No ordinary shopping trip would do. Stef had a very definite idea of where they needed to go—to see the Michael Jackson movie *This Is It*.

Stef already had seen the movie in October. She, Sue, and Myra went on Myra's birthday, reliving the fun they had years earlier when, as a high school cheerleader, Stef reveled in all things Michael Jackson. But now, with Cindy in town from California and Sandy back after a brief trip home to tend to her job in Florida, Stef became adamant. "Cindy and Sandy have to see the Michael Jackson movie."

Sue tried to talk her out of it. After all, it took a lot of effort to get Stef dressed and chauffeur her around town in her condition. But she insisted. She also wouldn't have any of Sue's suggestion about wearing sweats to make it easier. "I'm wearing my skinny jeans," Stef said.

They tried to talk her out of that too.

"No," Stef said, "I'm wearing my skinny jeans."

So they wrestled her into her skinny jeans, she put on her makeup, and off they went to see Michael Jackson.

Back in the fall of 1984, Stef's dad had taken a day off from his medical practice to drive to Cleveland on a special mission. He stood in line all afternoon—no doubt wearing his ever-present coat and tie—among thousands of moonwalkers and sequined-glove-wearing fans. That October, when the Jacksons' Victory Tour came to Municipal Stadium, somewhere in the crowd of 47,000 sat a slightly uncomfortable, but nevertheless proud, dermatologist, his wife—herself a former Rockette and June Taylor Dancer—and their four screaming daughters.

The Belcher girls apparently never got over their love for the King of Pop, because twenty-five autumns later, here they sat in a theater in Columbus, Ohio, rocking out to Michael Jackson's music and dancing, just as they had a quarter century before.

As Sue drove the crew back to our house that night, she looked over and said, "Stef, I can't believe you just did that."

Stef winked at her and said, "Never underestimate your little sister."

It was November 10, and I'm sure in heaven, Dr. Richard Belcher smiled, looking down at his girls on what would have been his seventy-third birthday.

That night and the experience at Noah's play gave Stef a burst of energy that carried her through the first part of November. Inevitably, though, her energy soon began to fade. Dr. Shapiro had encouraged me in October to make contact with hospice about attending to Stef's needs as we drew closer to the end. I resisted at first, but I knew in my heart that I needed to follow his advice. Her sisters and I had cared for Stef throughout the spring and summer. We did the best we could; I like to think we did very well. But none of us had the training, let alone the emotional strength, to walk the final steps without professional help.

Involving hospice was absolutely the right decision. They came at the beginning of the month and knew just how to make Stef the most comfortable. They also gave me a book that prepared me for what would happen. I struggled to read it and process the information, but I preferred to know the signs and behavior that would precede her dying, rather than get blindsided. One of the warning signs — her appetite stopping — already had taken place. A second, extreme fatigue, also had set in.

Sue saw the time getting close. She had one last important thing to discuss with Stef. She wanted to talk about our kids, about how much she loved them and how she would care for them in Stef's absence. Stef already knew that. How could she not know it, having witnessed all Sue did for our family over the years? But Sue needed to say it for her own peace of mind. When I sensed the right moment one day, I motioned for Sue to have that conversation.

"Stef," Sue said, "I want you to know …"

"Susan!" Stef stopped her. It was as if Stef were saying, "Don't state the obvious to me." But then she realized what this meant to Sue and so she let her finish.

I think Sue probably wanted a final good-bye, but in Stef's mind, this wasn't good-bye. She knew she would see us all again. She didn't need any dramatic discussions or final parting words at the end.

Stef had complete peace with what would happen and where she would be going. I thought she might not last much longer, because she slept so soundly at night and spent most of her day taking extended naps. I thought perhaps her time with us would just slowly wind down until she gradually faded away.

But instead, she surprised me again.

On Monday, November 16, Stef insisted on taking a shopping trip to Target with her mom and sisters.

"I have some pictures I need to get developed," Stef said.

Sue teased her about wanting to go simply to ride the scooter around the store. Sure enough, Stef got on and started plowing through the racks of clothes, looking for some winter nightgowns and some things for the kids. She remained very particular about what she bought. She still cared. She still wanted to be Stef, right down to the last detail.

Myra mentioned that she needed a new winter coat, so that became Stef's mission. She drove all over the women's department, looking for a coat for her mom. Only later did Sue and Sandy realize what Stef kept pointing at. "I found Mom's coat," she kept saying. Her sisters couldn't understand her. By that time, her speech had become very difficult to understand.

On the way home, Sue looked at Stef and all the things she bought and said, "Stef, I can't believe you had that in you. You spent $120 at Target. You literally shopped until you dropped."

Stef smiled, raised her hand in the air for a high-five, and said, "Yeahhhh."

WORDS OF WISDOM

THROUGHOUT NOVEMBER, STEF REPEATEDLY ASKED SUE THE SAME question: "When is Emily's birthday?"

Emily, like Sue's other daughters—Lauren, Allie, and Maggie—had a special relationship with Stef.

Once, during a particularly difficult time for Lauren, Stef called and asked if she would like to ride along to Kroger. Lauren knew her aunt well enough to sense this would be no routine shopping trip. Stef used the time to ask Lauren about some hurtful rumors circulating about her, spread by classmates at her high school. Girls at that age can be vicious, and these girls really did a number on Lauren's self-esteem. No matter how much a parent tries to repair the damage, sometimes it takes encouragement from someone else to get a teenager over the hump.

Stef and Lauren never made it into the store that night. They sat in the Kroger parking lot and talked. Lauren was surprised to learn that Stef had struggled with the same thing in high school when a group of girls bullied her. Her complete identification with Lauren's situation helped to reduce the enormity of the problem and made it something Lauren could manage and overcome. She had known Stef only as this completely together, confident woman. To hear that someone as mentally strong as Stef could be hurt by the same things made a tremendous impression on Lauren.

They talked for a long time and eventually wound up back at our house, in the driveway. They sat and talked for a while longer and Stef said to her, "If I had to go through what I went through just so I could help you deal with this now, then it was all worth it to me."

They cried quite a few tears together. The admiration Lauren had for Stef helped her realize that everyone goes through trials, including some that we don't deserve or create. Lauren hadn't failed or fallen short. Stef helped her understand the sad reality that some people are just mean and spiteful, and that those people need love and grace the most.

That put everything into perspective for Lauren. She came away from that night realizing she could stand strong because Stef had stood strong against the same challenge. According to her mom, Lauren became a different person from that night forward.

But now Stef's attention had shifted to Emily. And the date of Emily's birthday seemed to really bother Stef.

"When is Emily's birthday?" she kept asking Sue.

"November 18," Sue told her.

"When?"

"November 18."

We finally figured out why Stef had such a strong interest in the date. She wanted to make sure she would not die on Emily's birthday.

The eighteenth came and went two days after the sisters' final shopping trip to Target. Stef slept most of that Wednesday, like she had on Tuesday.

Thursday morning, I noticed a glassy look in her eyes and a further deterioration in her ability to speak. I called the hospice nurse.

"I think it's coming," I said.

The nurse came to our house and, after examining Stef, confirmed my thoughts. Late that afternoon, Stef's breathing began to change, becoming more labored. I knew, from reading the book provided by hospice, what *that* meant.

The kids came home from school around 3:30. Sue, Sandy, Cindy, and their mom had already arrived. They each got a final moment with Stef before she slipped away to heaven at 5:30. Her sisters and mom gave us some time alone in the room with Stef after she died. I said a prayer—not a sad prayer, but a prayer of thanksgiving.

"Mommy is free from cancer now," I said. "She is dancing and singing and her hair is beautiful. She's free. That's something we praise You for, Lord."

For as long as I could remember, I had prayed for God's mercy. I learned that His mercy doesn't always come how you think it will. I continually asked for mercy for Stef, wanting her to be healed. The night we learned the cancer had spread to her spine, I went in the kids' rooms and prayed for mercy that would spare them the grief of losing their mom. Instead of curing Stef on earth, God took her home for the ultimate healing. Instead of sparing our kids the pain of losing her, God gave them a shield of protection and the resilience to deal with her death.

Maddie, Noah, Macy, and Audrey said their good-byes to Stef before I loaded her body onto the stretcher and helped the funeral personnel take her out to the hearse. I kissed her one final time.

The kids had become very emotional by the time I came back into the house. But the way they handled it the rest of that night and in the coming days fell right in line with how Stef would have wanted them to handle it. They showed considerable strength and dignity in the face of great adversity and pain. They could have melted down emotionally, but they didn't. They watched everything. They participated in everything. I wanted them to take ownership of the experience and feel a part of it, down to the last detail.

Ultimately, I hope they can look back on Stef's passing, draw strength from it, and apply what they learned to whatever other difficult circumstances life presents them. I know it encouraged me and inspired me to watch them in that moment and during the rest of the night. They began really celebrating their mom, taking an active role in selecting the pictures and the music that we would feature at the memorial service on Tuesday. Audrey and Macy danced around as the music played, telling some of their favorite stories about Stef.

The next morning, I woke up just after 5 a.m., knowing I had something extremely important to find. Stef and her friend Heather Pick had visited our cabin in the Hideaway Hills in the summer of 2008, near the end of Heather's nine-year battle with breast cancer.

Stef and Heather had more in common than sharing a disease. Cancer struck Heather, like it did Stef, as a young mother. Heather was twenty-nine; Stef was thirty. Both of them majored in journalism in college. Heather, like Stef, had two children after learning she had breast cancer. And, like Stef, Heather used her public platform to raise money for cancer research.

Heather died almost exactly one year before Stef, on November 7, 2008. Her text messages remained on Stef's phone to the very end. Stef kept every text Heather ever sent her. Stef lost a lot of very dear friends to cancer, but Heather's death took the greatest toll on her. The two connected because they shared a high-profile standing in the community and therefore could understand, better than anyone else, the enormous demands and challenges each of them faced.

When Heather and Stef went to the cabin, Heather ran the camera while Stef recorded a video message to our family to be played if, and when, she died.

Now, the morning after Stefanie's death, I didn't know where she'd put that tape. I thought and thought. Hours passed until, about noon, it finally hit me. "The safe. It's probably in there." Sure enough, I found it, right in front, with a note that said: "For my family."

I gathered the kids and told them what I'd found.

"Let's watch it," I said.

Stef started by reassuring us. "I am somewhere unbelievably wonderful right now. I believe that. I believe that is where I'm going. And I want you to with all your hearts as well. I am OK. I am so OK, and you're going to be OK too. You really are. God is crying with you right now. He's wrapping his arms around you. He's holding you, and He wants you to give your burdens to Him. I trust God's plan, and I hope right now you are trusting God's plan." She shared her favorite Scripture, Jeremiah 29:11: "'For I know the plans I have for you,' declares the LORD, 'plans to prosper you and not to harm you, plans to give you hope and a future.'" One of the coolest things she did was to address each one of our children individually about what made them special. She told each one that she had prayed for their future spouse for a very long time. That made an incredible impression on them. She and I talked often about our goals for our kids, one of which involved finding a loving Christian mate. It amazed me she had the foresight to focus on that issue so far in advance.

She also talked to the kids about me. She talked about her expectations for them, about never using her death as an excuse for anything, but as motivation for everything. She talked to them about recognizing their faults and encouraged them to push through those difficulties. And last, she talked about how much she loved them and would miss seeing them grow up.

The tape lasted about forty-five minutes. We struggled through parts of it when our emotions got the better of us. It wasn't easy to watch, but we all wanted to watch it. The kids had painful memories of Stef because of the way cancer beat her up over the final nine months of her life. The healthy Stef on the tape had a voice that sounded bright and clear. Her eyes had that engaging warmth. I think she wanted us to watch it right away. After we did, I knew we'd made the right decision.

Maddie retreated to her room after the tape ended. I waited for a while and then went to check on her. I sat next to her on the bed and tried to comfort her as she cried. After a few minutes, she said, "Dad, I forgot." I knew right away what she meant. She had forgotten how Stef looked, how she sounded, how she could relate so well to her children when her mind functioned properly.

"I know, sweetheart," I said. "I forgot too. It's OK. That's why we have that, so we don't ever forget again."

Later that afternoon, I took some time to listen to a portion of the radio show I'd been doing in Columbus for several years. The day before the Ohio State–Michigan game typically means start-to-finish detail on every aspect of the rivalry. But on this day, no one wanted to talk about the game. The entire program consisted of calls from people wanting to express their memories of Stef and their condolences to our family.

I always knew Stef had connected with the community in a special way. But as I listened, the depth of the caring and the priority people placed on trying to comfort us really touched me. A friend text-messaged me during the show. "I know you think you know how much you mean to people. But, until today, I don't think you could ever really know how much you've meant to so many." That said it perfectly. Many of the callers were in tears, and some of the emails read on the air moved me to tears.

One in particular helped me realize that, while I had known Stef for twenty-seven years—twenty as her husband—I still didn't know some things about her. The email read:

I met Stefanie Spielman at the Ohio State hospital while awaiting tests in regard to my traumatic brain injury. We were in the waiting room. I looked across the aisle and Stefanie was there. I noticed she had come to the hospital with IV needles and tubes in her arm. I asked her if she was, in fact, Stefanie Spielman. She replied that she was.

We made some small talk. During this time, there was a young mom with three children there. The kids were being kids, playing and being quite rambunctious. The mother tried her best to keep them under control, but it was obvious that she was worn down and barely coping.

Stefanie gently talked to the children and asked them if they wanted something to play with. She then dug into her purse and retrieved some toys. She gave one to each child and set them up at a table to play. The young mother was so relieved, because her children played happily after that.

Trying to be cute, and because I was not mentally there at the time, I asked Stefanie if she had anything in her purse for me. She laughed and retrieved a red rubber ball and gave it to me. She laughed and told me not to get in trouble in the waiting room. I told her I was kidding, and that I really didn't want a toy. She had spoken to my wife about my situation, so Stefanie told me that I needed the toy far more than she did.

I kept that ball with me and carried it as a symbol of hope, determination and the complete selflessness of another. I carried that ball with me to all of my treatments while I recovered.

Last winter, a friend and co-worker went on the Buckeye Cruise for Cancer. I gave the ball to him and sent a letter describing the time

*Stefanie gave it to me. I told her that I carried the ball a lot since we
met. After she gave it to me, I carried it in my pocket for many of
my rehab treatments. I told her how much it meant to me and the
inspiration it gave to me. In the letter I thanked her and told her that
I was nearly back to normal, that it was now time to return the ball
and hopefully inspire her.*

*Stefanie cried tears of joy and compassion upon reading my letter.
She also took the time to contact me and inquire about my recovery.
This woman is and always will be a hero and an inspiration to me.*

*She could have stepped back in the hospital, being tired and worn
down while coping with chemotherapy. But instead, she took the
time to help a mom in need, struggling with her children. She could
have discounted as irrelevant this man she didn't know. Instead, she
inquired of my wife about my condition and made personal contact
with me.*

This was a great woman, great mother and great human being.

*"Never surrender" is a saying we put on the door of our football
locker rooms. Stefanie Spielman and her husband, Chris, certainly
epitomize that dynamic.*

*Heaven is certainly a richer place today. May God bless the
Spielman family in this time of sorrow. We all need to remember
to celebrate this great woman's life.*

Stef's humility kept her from telling me that story and many others
that people shared in the coming days. By holding on to those secrets,
she gave us a very unique gift at just the right time. Had we known
every instance of how she had touched people so deeply, we wouldn't
have experienced the joy of those special moments that gave us such
comfort when we needed it most.

That night, I visited the funeral home. They had a room set up for
me to be with Stef one last time. The night before, when she passed
away, I had a very emotional moment when they asked if I wanted to
remove her wedding ring as they prepared to take her body from our
house. I told them, "I can't do that yet." Waiting didn't make it any
easier. I got emotional again as I removed the ring. I sat with her body,
holding her hand, telling her how much I loved her. I knew that really

wasn't her lying there. It was just a shell. I knew her spirit was living in heaven and that she was looking down on me. I knew she didn't want me to feel so sad.

I told her not to worry. "I'm going to do everything you expect me to do, and I'm going to try to do it better than you expect me to do it." Then I wheeled her body into the crematorium, lifted her up onto the machine and pushed the button.

I wanted to be the one to do that. Stef was my wife. We'd walked a long and hard road over the last twelve years. We battled every step of the way, but the struggle grew our love in immeasurable ways. After going through all that together, I wanted to see the story through to the end. In a strange way, I didn't want her to be alone at that moment. And so we finished the race together.

CHAPTER 24

An Outpouring
of Love

Now that Stef had gone home to heaven, we faced a host of important and difficult "firsts" as a family. One of them came on Sunday morning, when we attended church for the first time since her death.

Brian Jones, a pastor at Trinity, preached his sermon on 2 Timothy 4:6–8, written by the apostle Paul near the end of his life: "The time for my departure is near. I have fought the good fight, I have finished the race, I have kept the faith. Now there is in store for me the crown of righteousness, which the Lord, the righteous Judge, will award to me on that day—and not only to me, but also to all who have longed for his appearing."

"I never cease to be amazed by God's timing," Brian began. "We actually picked out that Scripture to be read today about three months ago."

The service became, in many ways, a tribute to Stefanie. I didn't expect that. It caught me off guard in a very beautiful way. All the people who approached the kids and me afterward offered us a lot of comfort, which made us feel very special and loved.

By Sunday afternoon, I started running on adrenaline. My heart began pounding like it always did for an intense workout. I had assigned people jobs for the memorial service and calling hours, so I stayed busy checking on those details. People responded in such a tremendous way. I started going through everything necessary for things to come off just right. "OK, that's done. What's next?" I put a huge premium on trust and loyalty. Jen McDonald from Stef's Fund offered to take care of the calling hours, so I crossed that off my list, knowing it would get done.

Monday, everyone in our family got excited when my brother, Rick, and his family flew into town. Rick arrived just in time for the calling hours with Noah and me. Ohio State allowed us to use the Longaberger Alumni House, a facility we knew could handle the large crowd we expected. I wanted to give everyone who wanted to pay tribute to Stefanie a chance to do just that. We had scheduled it from 1 to 8 p.m., but we actually started at 12:45 because a line already had started to grow.

Everyone who came through the doors received a pink rose. We also had pink bracelets for them, like we'd sold at Kroger to raise money for the fund. Jen decorated the hallways with big pictures of Stef and set up videos of her giving some of her best speeches. The room where we greeted people had huge photographs of our family in the happiest of times. Many of those who came to express their condolences had never met Stef even once. The outpouring of support and appreciation caught me unprepared. Some people came in suits and ties, others in jeans, a few in Ohio State gear. One couple even wore their Massillon Tigers' jerseys. The entire Ohio State football team came through the line and presented me with the commemorative helmet they wore in the win over Michigan on Saturday. The helmet had my number, 36, on the side, and the pink Buckeye leaf with the initials "SS" on the back that all the players wore in tribute to Stef.

I heard more stories about Stef—things she had done for people, how she inspired them—that she never told me.

That made me feel very proud, but it also made me wonder: *Was I a good enough husband to her?* More importantly, it made me realize the extreme blessing of being a part of her life. Stef had probably fifteen to twenty people who might describe themselves as her close friend. She had a unique way of making everyone near her feel exceptional. I thought about that gift and about the times I made that observation about her. She usually reacted by smacking me in the shoulder in a playful way. She felt I gave her too much credit. It embarrassed her to get compliments for living how she felt compelled to live as a believer in Christ.

Noah wanted to stay with me the entire time at the calling hours. He really took ownership of the situation, which I thought showed incredible maturity for a thirteen-year-old. For him, it was the best way to deal with his mother's passing.

Rick stayed right by my side too. As my big brother, he always had that natural protective instinct. My sophomore year of high school, some guy started messing with me at basketball practice. Rick, a senior, saw the kid hit me with a cheap-shot elbow. Out of nowhere, Rick came flying in and just flattened the guy. He laid him out and then pushed him out through the gym doors. I never doubted that Rick had my back in every way.

Rick never stepped away once during the calling hours. At one point, someone offered him a protein bar. "I can't eat that," he said. "If Chris isn't eating, I can't eat." Having him there gave me tremendous comfort.

I got similar comfort from the messages people wrote on memory cards about the impact Stef had on their lives. Many who had never met her in person nevertheless wrote passionately about how she touched them from afar. Little children who had Stef as a choreographer in school plays scrawled heartfelt messages to our kids. Friends who knew the daily struggles of our fight shared poignant thoughts about the dignity she showed enduring the challenges cancer threw at us. And survivors paid tribute to the inspiration they drew from Stef's battle.

One card read:

Being a part of the fight against breast cancer with Stefanie made me all that much stronger. I'll never forget and will always be guided by her smile, bravery, optimism, courage, care, drive and determination. It's our turn to make her legacy have a life of its own.

I knew Stef had lived a powerful life. I expected some of this outpouring of affection. But I couldn't have anticipated the depth of the feelings her death inspired, nor the difference she made to people with no connection to the cancer world. One man wrote:

> *You unknowingly inspired a father of two autistic children to make a difference. God bless you for changing the life of a farm kid from Ohio.*

When eight o'clock came, more than two thousand visitors had gone through the line to express their condolences. I felt tired from standing for seven hours, but I left the alumni house far more inspired than exhausted. I knew I'd made the right decision to give people this opportunity. Whatever it did for them, it did far more for me and my kids to see how deeply Stef had touched people with the way she lived her life.

CHAPTER 25

THAT'S WHY I'M HERE

I WOKE UP AT 3:25 A.M. ON TUESDAY AND GOT IN A QUICK WORK-out. I spent some time in prayer. I'd given hundreds of speeches over the years, but this one meant far more to me than any of those. I wanted to be strong that morning for Stef's memorial service and what I would say about her. I wanted to send the main message that her life had portrayed: a message of hope, faith, and encouragement. I didn't want to "doom and gloom" anything.

After breakfast, we gathered Stef's extended family and mine for a short drive to the cemetery for a brief graveside service. It lasted only ten or fifteen minutes. Then we headed for the church and the memorial service.

I spent about twenty minutes in the basement, just getting my thoughts together. My nervous energy and heightened anticipation gave me a familiar edginess, the kind I used to have before a big game. This, though, had much more riding on it. I wanted the service to encourage people for the rest of their lives. I focused intently on making sure I said precisely the right words, and, most importantly, exactly what Stef would have wanted me to say. I didn't write down anything. I felt God would speak through me. I had complete peace and assurance that He would answer that prayer.

The service began with a ten-minute video of Stef, part of which we took from the tape she made for our family. It featured music and pictures picked out by the kids and Stef's sisters. A praise band sang some of Stef's favorite songs. My brother, Rick, read from John

14:1–6, 27. Sue's husband, Bill, read from 2 Corinthians 5:1–5 and Revelation 21:3–4.

Then came my turn.

I started with what Stef had asked me to do when we spoke about her memorial service in the hospital, after we found out the cancer had spread to her spine. She asked me not to talk about her, but to thank everyone for what they did for us.

"I'm going to start with The James family," I said. "What special people you are, and the mission that we are on. Not only are you my family, you are my teammates. So the message from her is, 'Today we celebrate; tomorrow we fight. And it starts again.'"

I also made sure to thank Stef's family, her mom and sisters and their families, for sacrificing so much to help us care for Stef and to do the things around the house she could no longer do:

I'm going to start with Myra, my mother-in-law. She doesn't know this, but people ask me how I get the strength that I have or how Stefanie got the strength that she had. Besides our good Lord, the strength came from Myra, as she went through a very similar situation when her husband died of cancer. I can't tell you how many times at night when I was feeling down or weak that I remembered you and your strength in dealing with your husband.

To Cindy for dropping everything to come and be with us. The last couple of weeks that you spent were memorable to Stef and certainly times that I cherish.

To Sandy, what a gift you've given our family. From the time you took off work to live with your mom and be over every day. The best thing to know, Sandy, and I want you to take this home: As soon as you walked into the room when Stef was in bed, you saw her face light up. You were her baby sister, and she adored you.

To sister Sue, what can I say? From day one, the night we went to the emergency room on March 1 until I came home from the emergency room at 4:30 in the morning, you were there. You have been there every single day since. You have sent a message of service to your four lovely children, to my lovely children, of what it's like to give without question and without expecting anything in return. You were a model sister, and you set the tone.

I thanked my mom and Rick:

There were many nights I sat up. I'd look at the mirror. I would walk around and I would think of my mom. I thought of my mom with great confidence, knowing that at home, she was sitting on a chair, praying, just like she was when I grew up in her house. I counted on that. I used that.

To Rick, my brother, who has always been there ... I don't know if I can say anything to you. I know it's a given. That's the greatest comfort I can have.

And then I reflected on Stef:

My wife was everything you could imagine. I told my kids how lucky and blessed I was to find my true love and spend twenty-five years with her. I am honored to have been able to do that. I am so blessed, that the one soul mate that God made for me, I spent twenty-five years with her, and twenty of them married. That's what I hold on to. I know, because I have the eternal perspective that this lifetime is a blink of an eye, that I will see her very soon.

I talked about all of Stef's passions in life—her family, fighting cancer, me—but I wanted everyone to know what truly ranked as her top priority:

Her number one passion in life was not to impose her faith on anybody, but to absolutely expose where that light came from. That was her mission. She was the light. She never apologized for it. She let her actions speak louder than her words.

I knew it would be much more powerful if I could show how Stef truly demonstrated that priority in the way she lived. Her selfless nature gave me plenty of examples, including the time I walked in on her at 2:30 in the morning while she prayed over our computer:

"What are you doing?" I said.

"I'm praying for this lady who sent an email to 'Ask Stefanie' on the JamesCare website. She was just diagnosed."

That was what she was. And she was like that every day, all day. The thing about it is, she never looked at it like God gave her cancer. She looked at it like God allowed her cancer for a reason. Looking around here today, she did not die in vain.

I also told one of the stories about Stef that I never knew until she died. A lady who came through the line at Stef's calling hours gave me a letter she had written to the editor of her local newspaper telling about an experience she had with Stef. The letter read:

In November 2006 I was diagnosed with breast cancer on my 50th birthday. A mastectomy followed 10 days later, followed by chemotherapy, radiation and reconstruction. In the week after my diagnosis, I attended a YWCA Woman to Woman event at the Aladdin Shrine Temple, a gathering of 1,000-plus women to support efforts to end homelessness in Columbus. I either left my seat early or returned afterward to reclaim something. I don't really remember, except that the lobby was completely empty, with the exception of a beautiful woman, standing and waiting, holding a pink umbrella. I knew it was Stefanie. I walked up to her. I introduced myself and told her of my upcoming surgery. She asked about my doctors, about my children, about how I was coping, and my upcoming treatments—all with a gentle smile on her face. As my tears appeared, she reached for my hand and said, "You'll be OK." My words quit tumbling and I apologized for bothering her. I will never forget what Stefanie said to me. "Don't you understand? That's what I'm here for." I felt strangely calm as I waited those next days for my surgery.

That lady's letter perfectly characterized my wife, how she lived and how she viewed her mission. I wanted everyone at Stef's memorial service and those watching at home on TV to understand the most important lesson of her life:

The thing to celebrate today is that she was so blessed that she understood what God had exactly in store for her. And she lived that.

What a blessed life! There was no confusion, but to be a light, and she used to celebrate that God was using her to help and serve, no matter who.

Let me share one verse with you, because people ask me, "How does she have so much peace?" I want to share the secret with you. Philippians 4:6 and 7: "Do not be anxious about anything, but in every situation, by prayer and petition, with thanksgiving, present your requests to God. And the peace of God, which transcends all understanding, will guard your hearts and minds in Christ Jesus."

That's her strength, folks. That's where she got it. That's where I get it. And I got it even more from her because she was my light. She was my example.

I closed with my final good-bye to Stef and what I know she wanted to leave with everyone:

I'm not a poet, but Friday morning on November 20, I woke up at 5:16. I looked at the clock. I wanted to mark the first day that I woke up without my wife. I started talking to Stefanie. I went into the room. I sat in the brown chair that we shared. This is what I said to her:

> *Pacing your room, it's late at night,*
> *Amazing to watch, you continue to fight.*
> *Your smile, your touch, two of many things I will miss,*
> *Holding forever in my heart, November 19, our very last kiss.*
> *I see you with our Lord, wrapped in his embrace,*
> *He says, "My sweet child." You are filled with his grace.*
> *She is free from the burdens of this life,*
> *Oh, the joy in my heart. You're home, my beautiful wife.*
> *I heard her say, "Daddy, how I missed you."*
> *He said, "Stef, my little girl. Let me hold you."*
> *The saints of heaven, they all begin to dance and sing.*
> *Welcome, Stefanie. All of heaven's bells begin to ring.*
> *Grabbing your crowns, laying them at Jesus' feet,*
> *"It was all for you, Lord. Cancer we beat."*
> *Fear is gone, nowhere to be found.*
> *Love and peace everywhere, all around.*

Honoring your wish, I will celebrate,
Knowing one day, you will greet me at heaven's gate.

She loved you all very much. You strengthened her. Thank you. Thank
you very much. May the Lord bless you all.

With those words, I think, I got the message out that Stef wanted
people to hear. I hope I honored her.

Emily, Sue's daughter—the niece whose birthday we believe Stef
made a special effort to stay alive for—followed with a touching song
titled "For Good." She did a marvelous job that definitely honored the
aunt who loved her and her sisters so much.

A member of our extended family said afterward that the service
motivated them to reevaluate what they believe. Could someone's life
really be changed by the message of a ninety-minute ceremony?

I hoped that it could.

I prayed that it could.

CHAPTER 26

THE NEW NORMAL

I HAD THREE QUALITIES AS A LINEBACKER THAT I WOULDN'T HAVE traded for anyone else's abilities in the same category. First, my vision. Second, my understanding of what other teams wanted to accomplish. Third—and this ranked first in what made me successful as a player —my instincts. I trusted my instincts more than anything else.

I'm still applying and relying on my instincts now, not in a football sense, but as a parent. I have a tremendous amount of trust in those instincts, because I believe they are God-inspired and God-given.

A friend asked me shortly after Stefanie's death if I had put down one heavy baton—a twelve-year battle with breast cancer that eventually claimed her life—for the heavier burden of being a single dad. I don't consider this baton heavier because my children have a foundation of faith to support them. Managing our family is a lot easier than it would be for the single parent of a family without that foundation.

I've had to learn "on the run" in some ways. I try to make a special moment during the day for each of my children—maybe as brief as dropping Maddie off at school, talking to Noah about one of his games, or reading a book to Macy and Audrey. At some point every day, I try to give each one my full attention. I've become good at giving hugs out of the blue. I think they need them. I know *I* need them.

We lost Stef right before Thanksgiving in 2009, which made things more difficult for all of us. Stef put a heavy premium on family traditions, so not having her around to celebrate Thanksgiving and Christmas gave me an immediate dilemma. Should we keep all those traditions the same or change everything? I didn't want to make it tougher on my kids, doing things that reminded them of their mom. But I didn't want to discontinue those traditions if they would comfort them.

We talked about it and they unanimously agreed that they wanted to do everything the same. So we decorated just like always, visited the same farm for our Christmas tree, and made cookies like we would have if Stef had been here. It posed a challenge, because I found out grief doesn't fight fair. It comes when you least expect it and strikes without warning.

The most innocuous things—smells, pictures, songs, ornaments—all brought back memories that triggered emotions I knew would come and yet struggled to handle. I enjoyed the memories themselves, but it made me sad we couldn't share them with Stef. It brought home the sense of loss. I don't think anyone can understand the connection a loved one has to every single thing a family does until that person dies. That's when you find out how extensively they're woven into the fabric of even the things you don't automatically associate with them. Things like TV shows, little jokes, favorite foods, or places around town all had meaning for me and the kids because they all had a piece of Stef in them. With her gone, we began to understand the depth of her inclusion in every memory, every tradition, and every habit. Her absence left a hole in everything we once enjoyed so thoroughly. While that hurt lessened with time, I suspect it will never go away entirely.

Given that harsh reality, the kids did remarkably well adjusting to life without their mom. I think the distractions of Christmas, the parties and things, helped them. School started right afterward, so their minds remained occupied with something most of the time. They managed their grief and continued to function. The mercy of God kept the pain from overwhelming them. They didn't sink into depression, but I clearly sensed how much they missed her. They didn't bury their feelings or emotions. I thought they dealt with them in a healthy way. I realized from the way I felt that reaching our new normal would be a process we'd all have to work through.

At first, people struggled to know how to talk to us. Should they mention Stef, or should they avoid the topic to spare us pain? I understood, but talking about her and sharing their memories of her helped us. It worked the same way in our family. If any of my kids wanted to talk to me about Stef, I welcomed the opportunity. If not, I didn't push them. That option will always exist. We have to communicate, but we don't have to force that communication.

One of the little girls told her teacher soon after Stef died that she missed her mom, so I talked with her about it. "I hear you miss Mom," I said. "I miss her too. I miss her every day. But when I start missing her and I get sad, I think of the times that Mom made me laugh and some of the fun things we did. We're always going to miss Mommy. But we're going to try to remember the good times and how Mommy would want us to feel. It's OK to be sad." Once she heard me say that, and that I missed Stef too, it seemed to comfort her.

Another time one of my girls began to really struggle, just when I had to leave for work. I wanted her to remember how much Daddy cared for her, so of course I told her: "Daddy loves you very much. I will be back soon. I'm always here for you." And then I did something that maybe only a former football player would even think to do. I took a pen and wrote my words to her on her arm, in permanent ink. So she went to school looking like she had tattoos all over her arms. But for sure she knew that Daddy was indeed thinking about her — and it worked so well, I repeated the drill more than once.

I'm not alone in keeping watch. All four of my kids watch over *me* to make sure *I'm* OK. We're the consummate team. We watch each other's backs.

Early on, my youngest, Audrey, said, "Daddy, I feel bad for you."

"Why?" I asked.

"Because you always have to pack the lunches and cook our meals, and I know you liked to do stuff with Mom, and now you don't get to do those things anymore."

I told her, "That's OK. I like packing your lunches. I like cooking for you. It gives me a chance to help you."

Leading up to Stef's death, I didn't shy away from difficult conversations with the kids about what eventually would happen. Trying to prepare them was difficult, but I'm glad we had those talks. No one could ever fully prepare themselves for the loss of a loved one. The enormity of the pain doesn't hit until you actually lose the person. But it helps now when I can say to them, "Remember, we talked about this."

Two weeks after our first Christmas without Stef, I had hip-replacement surgery to correct a deteriorating condition dating to my years in the NFL. My mom came to town and took great care of the kids and me. I had to stay home for a week, unable to go anywhere because of my restricted mobility. During that week, the weight of the previous nine months collapsed on me. I spent every day in our library, the room where Stef spent most of her time in a hospital bed we rented after the cancer attacked her brain and spine.

It made me very sad, being in the room that reminded me of the last days of Stef's battle. The whole dynamic of my inability to walk, needing help, and relying on other people for my basic needs gave me a new perspective on what she must have endured. While my challenge didn't compare to Stef's, it gave me some insight into her mind-set during those final months.

I sure didn't relish going in there every day. But I didn't want to feel held captive to the impulse of refusing to go into the room where Stef spent most of her final months. I have all my books in that room. I like that room. I couldn't allow myself to remain frightened of that room forever. I needed to conquer that fear.

Unable to get out of bed or to tend to the kids' needs, I had no distractions to occupy my time and thoughts. I set up a chair next to where we placed Stef's bed and talked to her as if she were still alive. My grief hit me hard.

Until then, I hadn't allowed myself to face the recent past. Throughout the late summer and early fall, I'd focused on closely watching the kids to see how they coped. Planning for the end occupied so much of my time that I put off dealing with the pain I felt. Those memories ate away at me. I remembered Stef in the cancer-wracked condition of her final days, not as she was during her healthy years.

As I spent day after day in that room, it got easier. Instead of complete sadness every minute, I had some happy memories too. I thought about the great times we shared as high school sweethearts, the Ohio State years when we began falling in love, starting our life together as my NFL career took off, her modeling and TV success, the young and carefree lives we lived back then. I cherished those memories and they made me smile. They also made me sad, because I knew we would never share more times like that.

The more I thought about how much I loved her, the more I realized the tremendous blessing I enjoyed having her in my life. Of course, that made me miss Stef all the more. The delay in dealing with those thoughts until two months after she died, until after the holidays, might actually have helped me. I had time to build up the emotional strength to spend six or seven hours a day in that room and do some necessary grieving. If I had tried to do it any earlier, I might have suffered a complete breakdown.

I faced another emotional hurdle on my first trip to Stef's grave. I didn't go until January 19, two months after she died. I'll probably visit once a month for the rest of my life, probably on the nineteenth. I know she's in heaven, not in the cemetery. The gravesite just gives me a place to reflect, remember, and honor her.

Our vacation to Disney World the next March brought another hurdle. We went for the first time as a family in January 1999, after Stef finished her initial round of chemotherapy. Back then, Maddie was four and Noah was two. Macy and Audrey hadn't been born yet. I wondered if the older kids would get hit hard by memories of their earlier trip with their mom, or whether they wouldn't make the connection and just have fun. It turned out great. They had a blast and so did I.

My kids also blew me away that first summer without Stef during induction weekend for the 2009 College Football Hall of Fame class in South Bend, Indiana. The people behind the Buckeye Cruise for Cancer organized a motor coach tour for the weekend. More than a hundred Ohio State fans showed up for the parade and ceremonies on the steps of the Hall of Fame, all of them wearing Spielman No. 36 Ohio State jerseys with the Stefanie Spielman Fund patch on the front. The number of people who came to support me that weekend really humbled me. Initially, I wanted to share that experience only with my family. It ended up as a family celebration. I just had a much larger family—the Ohio State family, which I'm proud to belong to.

Once the other Hall of Fame inductees saw all those people in my jersey, they really gave it to me. "Seriously, dude. What is *wrong* with those people?" The OSU fans just took over the parade route. I felt so appreciative and grateful to experience something so unique and special, something I will remember for the rest of my life.

Saturday night at the dinner for inductees, the organizers asked if they could interview my kids on stage. I left it up to Maddie and Noah, and they decided to do it. I think widows and widowers always worry, "How are my kids handling this?" I didn't know how they would answer or if they could maintain their composure.

They both talked about their mom and what she meant to our family. They really did her proud that night—the night before Stef would have turned forty-three. Maddie told the audience, "My mom would always say, 'No doom and gloom.' So, I'm sure she would want this day to be nothing but a celebration."

That was the best part of the weekend for me, seeing how our children handled everything. I don't want to take away anything from the honor of getting inducted into the Hall of Fame, but watching Maddie and Noah on stage with a microphone, speaking eloquently about their mother, topped everything else that weekend.

The induction weekend came one day before the eight-month anniversary of Stef's passing. To watch my children handle life— when things go well and when they don't, when grief can strike at any moment—and see them maintain balance and perspective, while continuing to move forward, gave me the greatest honor any father could ever receive.

What they've done has built upon the legacy of their mother and what she stood for all those years as she fought through repeated cancer battles, always thinking of others and what she could do to inspire and encourage people. We tried very hard to instill that lesson in our children, so I'm extremely gratified to see it play out that way.

I've come to realize I don't need to fear family events and special celebrations. I don't need to wonder if those things will throw my kids into a funk because Stef is no longer with us. My kids have demonstrated over and over that they are strong enough to do what they used to do with their mom, without getting leveled by the memories.

EPILOGUE

OCTOBER 2011

I MADE A PROMISE TO STEFANIE SHORTLY BEFORE SHE DIED. I took her hand in mine, looked in her eyes, and said, "I promise you, with every fiber of my being, that I will carry on this fight in your name. As long as I have a breath, I will never stop. I promise you that."

Maddie and Noah have also accepted that challenge. They asked if they could join me on stage at Champions in April 2010 to present the awards to the caregivers we honored. That event raised $120,000 for the fund, which put it at $7.3 million since its inception in 1998. A year later, with Maddie and Noah on stage as presenters once again, we topped $8 million. In October 2011, the fund had risen to $9.1 million, and Ohio State honored Stef by renaming its breast cancer center the Stefanie Spielman Comprehensive Breast Center.

I have no doubt that with the example their older brother and sister have set for them, Macy and Audrey will follow in their mother's footsteps. We will all continue to participate in Champions, Race for the Cure, the Buckeye Cruise for Cancer, and other events because those things had such a special place in Stef's heart. We will remain involved as a way of honoring her.

I know God has placed His healing hand on each of my children. My greatest fear was always how they would react. But they've been amazing. They have responded better than anything I ever imagined, which I know can be traced to the strength God has equipped them with to go forward. He has used, and I'm sure will continue to use, people who knew Stef to comfort, encourage, and inspire our kids.

Soon after she died, we received a hardcover book from people who had attended elementary, junior high, and high school with Stef. It has numerous pictures of her growing up with her school friends and the stories they wrote about how Stef impacted their lives long before she had cancer.

Having breast cancer no doubt refined Stef's gifts and gave her a greater platform, but she always had a unique compassion for people. That message resonated throughout the book, particularly in this story from a guy she knew:

> *I was a confused, angry, awkward kid with a bad haircut, just looking for where I fit in. I remember how pretty and popular you were. I figured people liked you because of how attractive you were. The truth of the matter is, people liked you because you were nice to everyone, listened attentively and were very genuine. I remember how you treated others and I think I incorporated some of those qualities into the way I behaved. I wanted to be a better person and you were the example to follow.*

I could never say anything more eloquent to my children about following their mom's example than that. Page after page, story after story, Stef's friends wrote about who she was and how she acted, giving my kids a priceless set of memories they can always draw on.

The book included many other references to the impact Stef made on people's faith just by being herself. Even then, she had a unique gift for drawing others to Christ with the love and grace she exhibited in everything she did. Consider this story by another classmate:

> *I believe some of Jesus' best friends are called to suffer with and for Him for the salvation of others. It is a huge and, many times, unwanted cross. I think we'll understand it better when we get to heaven and see all the souls we positively affected. It is no surprise to me that Jesus called you to do this with Him. You have already positively affected so many people before the cancer, and now the number of people that you have had an impact on is incredible. I admire your strength and sacrifices through it. I hope you realize how much kindness you have brought to so many of us and how you have brought so many closer to Christ through your acceptance, hope, love and perseverance.*

My children and I cherish that book from Stef's friends. That book and the hundreds of cards and letters we received after her passing give us a life preserver whenever the sadness of her death threatens to overwhelm us.

Stef would have celebrated, hearing that her death caused people to reexamine what faith can do in their lives. The letters served as a blessing and a validation from God, saying, "You did make a difference. Your faith did not waiver. For that, I'm going to show you the fruits of your labor in some of the lives you touched." That feels good, not in a self-serving way, but because it confirms in my heart that she didn't battle so long and so hard for nothing.

It also made me realize that all the time I spent in prayer—hours upon hours in my weight room at home, in the car, alone at night —had a significant purpose. I believe Stef's death will have an impact for eternity. I don't know how many victories God will win through his Holy Spirit acting on a seed Stef planted in someone's heart, but at least I know that we did a good job of exposing what we believe without imposing our faith on anyone.

When I feel sad or down, I read some of those letters and think, *What a glorious mission in life.* She did it so well. She was so genuine and kind. To be able to do that on a daily basis, without ever complaining or getting frustrated, still amazes me.

It really helps our family to openly talk about losing Stef—not in a negative way, but in a positive way. When we visit Stef's gravesite, the tears definitely flow. But sadness doesn't dominate our emotions. We talk about our memories of her, the times we laughed or learned something from her. We finish by having dinner at one of her favorite places. We end up feeling closer to her, not farther away.

I get asked a lot if the grieving process gets easier as time passes. I've found the moments of grief hit with every bit of the intensity that they did originally, but they don't come as frequently. So, does it get easier? No, but it's manageable.

I still miss Stef every day. I don't know when, or if, that feeling will ever disappear. Whenever I think back on our life together, I miss her a lot. I miss so many things, but most of all I just really, really miss my friend. I struggle with the reminders of what we shared. A song, a smell, a joke, a memory pops into your head and it makes you sad. It's not a depressed sadness, but a "man-do-I-ever-miss-her" sadness. People who have lost a loved one understand.

The kids have completely positive memories of Stef, which is a credit to her and the things she left them, like the video. I know they are missing something incredible, and they know they are missing something incredible, but they choose to live, as opposed to continuing to mourn.

Being a single dad sometimes makes me feel woefully inadequate, like I'm in a fight I can't win. I don't have enough time to do everything I want to do with my children. I probably will battle this feeling of inadequacy the rest of my life. I want to serve each kid the best I can, but I don't know how to make enough time for that. I'm sure many single parents battle the thought, *Am I giving enough attention here? Am I giving enough attention there?*

As an NFL football player, I evaluated myself every day: *OK, this is what I did well. This is what I need to improve on. This is what I stunk at.* I do the same sort of evaluation regarding my relationship with each child. In that sense, I sort of review the practice tape at the end of every day and grade myself as a father. My two primary missions in life are my children and keeping Stef's fund going to fight breast cancer. Both give me ample opportunity to honor Stef in the way that I promised her.

Most people at some point in life ask the question, "Why am I here?" Stef had a very clear understanding of the answer to that question. She had such confidence in her mission from God that she had no fear of the future. She understood her instructions and she followed them to the letter. Obviously, she wanted to find a cure for breast cancer, but her main driving force centered on encouraging and inspiring people to live lives of consequence and contentment. She did that every day. I don't know how she found the strength. Sometimes I would get overwhelmed, but she never did. I can't comprehend all the genuine love she had in her heart for everybody. It was remarkable to watch.

Fortunately, I get to see it every day reflected in the lives of our children. Stef left her mark on them—in their servant hearts and how they take care of each other. Ultimately, her death will bless them if they stay the course to become the kind of people that would make her proud.

That thought gives me such peace as we approach the future. As I watch them, I'm more convinced than ever that God is a good God. He gives us many blessings. It's easy to get caught up in continually looking for the next blessing, but when I look back and reflect on all the blessings my family already has received, I have zero doubt in my mind that God is very, *very* good.

These days, I offer up a lot more prayers of thanksgiving than prayers of petition. I don't ask for as many things as I once did. I have attained a level of contentment that I used to doubt I would ever achieve. I'm thankful for that. I'm thankful for how my kids have adjusted. I'm very aware of how blessed we are. As we approach the future, I have a profound sense of peace.

The first part of my life focused solely on winning, or trying to win. If I didn't win, it made me more obsessed to win the next time. Now I look at life differently. It's not what you accomplish that's most important. It's what you experience and overcome along the way. Instead of always looking for the end result, I've learned to embrace the journey.

Despite the outcome of Stef's battle, I consider myself very fortunate. I found my soul mate, the one I believe God created especially for me. We had a deep love affair for twenty-seven years. I consider that one of the greatest blessings ever lavished on me.

I look back and I realize that God prepared us for this specific moment in time and for this specific purpose. We went through the gamut together. We climbed mountains together that we never could have climbed alone. Our journey ended differently than we desired, but the memories and emotions will always be there to treasure. And what we learned while striving to walk with God will sustain our family forever.

AFTERWORD

My first meeting with Stefanie and Chris Spielman in 2001 is forever etched in my mind. Stefanie had received chemotherapy three years earlier, when she was first diagnosed with Stage II breast cancer at age thirty. In 2001, she developed a chronic cough that led to X-rays and a biopsy, which confirmed the cancer had spread to her lungs.

I tried my best not to appear anxious on that first visit. I knew that Stefanie and Chris were "local celebrities" who had made her breast cancer public and had created a fund for breast cancer research. I could tell Stefanie felt anxious, but she tried her best to put me at ease. I was struck by her warmth, friendliness, and unassuming manner. Chris tried hard to stay calm during our meeting. He asked most of the questions, frequently apologizing by saying, "I just need to understand this."

As we finished our discussion, Chris looked me straight in the eye and said, "I could have taken my wife anywhere in the country to receive the best care, but I choose to have her treated at The James. You're the quarterback now. Move the ball."

No pressure at all, I thought.

For twelve long (or, in some ways, short) years, Stefanie and Chris —as well as their children, extended family, and many in the Ohio State University family across Ohio and the United States—traveled a long and winding road. At times they faced extreme challenges, hardships, and obstacles, when every step seemed harder than the last. At other times the road grew easier, and the Spielmans could almost convince themselves things would be OK and that they could get back to normal.

Along this road, I served as guide, troubleshooter, and witness to their travels. But they also served as my inspirational teachers, although neither Stefanie nor Chris knew it. Even had I made them aware, I imagine they would have remained gracious, even if they felt puzzled at the notion they might be imparting valuable lessons to me.

Much of my professional life of more than twenty years as an academic breast cancer oncologist has involved writing grants and research papers. That's a big part of what I do when I'm not treating breast cancer patients. I thought writing my memories of Stefanie and Chris and their shared battle would be easy for me, given my writing experience. Instead, I found it much more difficult than I ever imagined, because their journey—like so many others I have witnessed —overflowed with such complex human experiences that I find it hard to select what to include and what should better be left unsaid. Nonetheless, I will try to get on with it and "move the ball."

This book told the story of Stefanie's battle, from Chris's point of view. I think of it also as a collection of love stories:

- The love between Chris and Stefanie.

- Selfless love to make Stefanie's breast cancer—for most, a very private matter—public, in order to raise awareness of the importance of screening mammography and to provide inspiration and hope to countless women living with breast cancer.

- Loving and honoring the caregivers, often forgotten, via Stefanie's Champions luncheons.

- And the Spielmans' love of God, given the underlying and central theme that religious faith and devotion played in sustaining them throughout Stefanie's treatments.

Consider this book a guide for selfless giving. Many aspire to live in such fashion, but few demonstrate it so openly and naturally in day-to-day living as Chris and Stefanie did.

True love is often messy. It encompasses the highest elements of ethical and moral behavior, attraction, sensuality, mutual respect, friendship, and the joy of bringing children into the world. But it also includes the pain, despair, frustration, anger, loss of control, and powerlessness of watching a loved one grow weaker each day, as Stefanie did until her final diagnosis in March 2009.

Chris related several stories to me over the years when I served as Stefanie's oncologist. I want to retell one of those stories from memory (which is not what it once was, and I take full responsibility for any inaccuracy in its retelling). This story in particular sticks in my mind:

As they drove to one of their first doctor appointments after her initial diagnosis of breast cancer, Chris drove fast (and admittedly a little unsafely), feeling tremendous anger over the news. He cursed at the world, which I have never heard him do in more than ten years. He felt frustrated with the diagnosis, seeing Stefanie's cancer as totally unfair because she had done nothing to deserve it. After a short time of listening to his ranting and raving, Stefanie commanded, "Stop the car right now and pull over!"

When he did, she declared, "I don't ever want to hear you talk like that again." No one deserves a cancer diagnosis, she said, adding that they had received many blessings as a family, and they had much to be grateful for. Stefanie considered the "Why me?" a waste of time and energy.

She had more important things to do.

First, Stefanie willingly participated in clinical trials. A clinical trial gives the best treatment possible, but in the context of asking a research question. Depending on the type of clinical trial, the question may concern how the newer treatment compares with the well-established treatment. Or it may evaluate a new experimental drug in terms of both its side effects and anti-cancer effects. Everything we know, or will know in the future, about how to best treat breast cancer comes as a direct result of the courageous women who have or will partner with their physicians and voluntarily participate in clinical trials.

Stefanie understood this. She saw it as a very meaningful way to contribute to "the fight." Although she recognized that she might not personally benefit from it, the knowledge gained from every clinical trial benefits future patients diagnosed with breast cancer. Stefanie used this as yet another way to selflessly give—a central theme in her life.

Second, the Stefanie Spielman Fund originally was set up as an endowment fund, in which only the interest generated on the total amount could be used for breast cancer research. Stefanie wanted the fund to support more than an endowment fund could generate, so we talked about how to best use the funds for breast cancer research. As a result, the fund currently supports human breast cancer tissue banks, which researchers use to advance discoveries about breast cancer and to successfully obtain funding from the National Cancer Institute and other federal funding sources. In addition, the fund supports a graduate student and technician in a lab devoted to discovering new drugs for breast cancer. It also finances an endowed professorship in breast cancer imaging research. But perhaps closest to Stefanie's heart, the fund provides money and resources for women with breast cancer and their families, such as a Thanksgiving dinner for families that cannot cook or afford one, or the purchase of a wig for a woman facing hair loss from chemotherapy treatments.

Stefanie and Chris blazed a trail for others. In 2002, Stefanie had just begun receiving trastuzumab (also called Herceptin) when she found out she was about fourteen weeks pregnant. At that time, we had virtually no experience with this drug administered during the first trimester of pregnancy, when all the fetus's organs start to form. We worried that the drug might damage the brain, heart, or other organs.

Stefanie and Chris faced three gut-wrenching options: discontinue the trastuzumab and put Stefanie at risk of worsening cancer; terminate the pregnancy; or continue to treat Stefanie with trastuzumab and monitor the fetus closely. Stefanie told me when she and Chris saw the baby's heart beating on the ultrasound, they knew what to do.

About six months later, after receiving trastuzumab throughout much of her pregnancy, Stefanie delivered a healthy baby girl. With her consent, a major oncology journal published her experience of receiving this drug during pregnancy (called a case report).

Faith—that's what Stefanie and Chris had. Not just *any* faith, but one so strong and palpable it almost seemed you could touch it. It surrounded them inside and out, without the slightest whisper of lingering doubts, uncertainties, or unanswered questions. Chris didn't talk about it much, and I don't recall Stefanie ever mentioning it to me. But it was always there, especially evident in the last days when Chris told me, "Stef has no fear. She is going to see her dad again (in heaven) and she will be beautiful, in perfect health. And when I go, she'll be waiting for me, and we will be together again."

Breast cancer oncologists enjoy a privileged position. We witness the inner strengths and resiliency of women and their families as they face their fears and uncertainties with grace and courage—a triumph of the human spirit over the most dire, gut-wrenching circumstances. Women, many for the first time, directly face their mortality without all the mechanisms that serve to insulate and protect us from the one certainty—that each of us is going to die.

Sometimes it goes another way. Families get pulled apart. Couples separate or divorce. Some women despair after the crisis of breast cancer when they see that life, even under the best of circumstances, is too short—and they realize how unfulfilled their own life feels.

I often have asked myself, "What is the lesson here? What have I learned from walking on this road and bearing witness?"

Stefanie and Chris served as my inspirational teachers, although, as I said, they didn't know it. They taught their lessons by example, as effortlessly and naturally as one breathes. It has been said that the highest form of charity occurs when the giver and receiver don't know each other, thus making any recognition or reward impossible. Stefanie and Chris clearly fit into the "selfless givers" category.

And all of us were the receivers.

This couple made their personal breast cancer experiences public, to provide hope and inspiration to multiple thousands of women. I cannot imagine how difficult this must have been. They used their celebrity to create a fund for breast cancer research that continues to make a difference today and ultimately will contribute toward developing new treatments for this disease. And they established Stefanie's Champions—with Chris as the first Champions recipient—to thank the caregivers, the unsung heroes who also selflessly give.

They did all this and so much more.

Selfless giving with gratitude and appreciation: this was not only their gift, but also, in a sense, their challenge. Adversity, confusion, pain—both physical and emotional—and loss also are central parts of life. Stefanie and Chris taught us how to meet these difficulties and find a way to turn the dark into light.

The night before Stefanie passed away, Chris said to me, "After she's gone, there's going to be a lot more work. To honor her memory and continue her legacy, I am totally committed to keep the fund going and growing. I don't want Maddie or my other girls having to face this."

Knowing Stefanie and Chris has enriched my life. For me, just to be in their presence and to see how they conducted themselves gives me hope and inspiration whenever I encounter the adversity and uncertainty of life and come face-to-face with my own demons. Chris continues on that journey, and I will remain by his side.

CHARLES L. SHAPIRO, M.D.
October 25, 2010